A CHATEAU IN
HESSMER
A COLLECTION OF SHORT PLAYS

DAVID J. HOLCOMBE

authorHOUSE®

AuthorHouse™
1663 Liberty Drive
Bloomington, IN 47403
www.authorhouse.com
Phone: 1 (800) 839-8640

© *2015 David J. Holcombe. All rights reserved.*

No part of this book may be reproduced, stored in a retrieval system, or transmitted by any means without the written permission of the author.

Published by AuthorHouse 01/15/2015

ISBN: 978-1-4969-6353-6 (sc)
ISBN: 978-1-4969-6352-9 (e)

Any people depicted in stock imagery provided by Thinkstock are models, and such images are being used for illustrative purposes only. Certain stock imagery © *Thinkstock.*

This book is printed on acid-free paper.

Because of the dynamic nature of the Internet, any web addresses or links contained in this book may have changed since publication and may no longer be valid. The views expressed in this work are solely those of the author and do not necessarily reflect the views of the publisher, and the publisher hereby disclaims any responsibility for them.

ACKNOWLEDGEMENT & DISCLAIMER

"A Chateau in Hessmer" contains a collection of short plays, many of them in a ten-minute format, although a few substantially longer. The subjects are grouped together by similar themes or subject matters.

Although the characters may sometimes seem familiar, any resemblance to the living or dead is strictly fortuitous. That being said, no author can remain insensitive to the astonishing array of people and situations that surround him or her. Some of the medical or political themes may shock, and, as such, in no way reflect the views of my current or past employers. All opinions and all responsibility for these works remain my own.

I would like to extend my heartfelt appreciation to the members of the Central Louisiana Writers Guild, an organization which has survived though the decades thanks to the dedication of a few amazing local writers. I would also like to thank the many playwrights, filmmakers and other creative individuals who have graced our home and shared their talents and experiences, however briefly.

Last, but not least, I would like to thank my long-suffering wife, Nicole, who has indulged my writing pretentions ("the money pit" as she calls it) for many years. Her razor sharp wit never ceases to amaze and edify me. She has, nonetheless, remained the bedrock of my life, without which I would have surely drifted away into the airless and lifeless stratosphere.

David J. Holcombe, M.D., M.S.A.
January 2015

"If a man does not keep pace with his companions, perhaps it is because he hears a different drummer. Let him step to the music which he hears, however measured or far away."

Henry David Thoreau

Contents

FOUR ARCHITECTURAL SKETCHES

BUILDING A CABIN

BUILDING A CASH COW

BUILDING THE TAJ MAHAL

BUILDING A CHATEAU IN HESSMER

BUILDING A CABIN

CAST OF CHARACTERS

JOHN: Middle-aged man casually dressed.

PETER: Middle-aged man casually dressed.

SETTING

Both men are seated or standing next to a table on which is located an architectural model of some sort of cabin. It can be constructed of foam board and needs to be easily identifiable as a building.

JOHN: Nice, very nice. Are those solar panels on top?

PETER: Yes, and the heating will be an on-demand tank-less heater, in addition to a fuel-efficient low-emissions, pellet burning stove.

JOHN: Aren't those tank-less heaters really expensive?

PETER: Yep! Top dollar. But they're worth it. You just heat the water you need when you need it, and not a whole huge water heater full all the time. And out back I'll have the organic garden and the free-range chickens and the composter. It'll be great!

JOHN: What does Mary think?

PETER: Mary?

JOHN: Yes, your wife Mary?

PETER: I thought you were talking about the Virgin for a minute. (*Laughs at his own lame joke.*) She's behind this project 100%. In fact, she's the one pushing this. She wants us to downsize, to simplify and focus on the essentials in life.

JOHN: Like Henry Thoreau?

PETER: Exactly, just like Thoreau, just like his cabin at Walden Pond, but with solar panels.

JOHN: What about your kids?

PETER: Greg's in college and Catherine's planning on moving to L.A. to become a movie star.

JOHN: Really? That sounds unrealistic.

PETER: (*Shrugs.*) What can we do? We gave her a solid secondary education and now it's up to her. We encouraged her to go to college, but she is damned and determined to go out West and become a famous actress.

JOHN: A bit young for that, isn't she?

PETER: (*Defensively.*) She wants her independence and says she'll fight for it whether we agree or not.

JOHN: Pete, (*Pauses. Puts his hand on PETER's shoulder*) you know that on average unattached young people in big cities get sexually exploited within 48 hours.

PETER: Not Cathy! She's going to have an apartment, a job, connections, and real prospects. She'll be protected. She's not some homeless runaway drug addict. She's a beautiful, intelligent, talented girl with a loving family.

JOHN: Forty-eight hours. That's the rule, at least for runaways. (*Pauses.*) We thought our son, Frank, had his head on his shoulders, too. But it only took a couple of years in Las Vegas to kill him.

PETER: I'm sorry. I remember hearing that.

JOHN: We wanted to be empty nesters and we wanted a little house in the country. But what we got was a body bag and a daily dose of grief that won't go away.

PETER: I'm so sorry?

JOHN: And what about your son, Greg? How is he doing in school?

PETER: Good, really good.

JOHN: Still pre-med, right?

PETER: Maybe, although we're hearing things about psychology or even art history, or sociology.

JOHN: Art history? I didn't know he was artistic.

PETER: Me neither. In fact, he's colorblind. (*Shows the cabin model.*) We'll also have an area out back for people who want to visit, where they can camp.

JOHN: No spare room?

PETER: Nope! On purpose. We want to be sociable, but it's such a nice location, we'd have a hoard of visitors, including relatives.

JOHN: (*Laughs.*) Yeah. (*Pauses.*) Greg's really studying art history? Really?

PETER: (*Angrily.*) Yes! Or maybe psychology, for what that's worth. We told him he could do anything he wanted, but he had to be able to earn a living and be independent when he finishes college.

JOHN: We told our Frank the same thing before he told us about his pregnant girlfriend and his failing grades and his drug problem.

PETER: Greg and Cathy aren't going to be like that. I swear to God!

JOHN: So did we. We swore to God and we prayed to God and then we paid for rent and child support and rehab and bail until we had to cut him off. The counselors at the rehab hospital said we were enabling and we probably were. He was going to have to sink or swim. (*Pauses.*) And then he died.

PETER: Why are you telling me this?

JOHN: We're friends. We grew up together. We're colleagues and yet I don't really even know you and your family.

PETER: If you bring a tent, you can camp out back for a week or so and you might get to know us a bit better.

JOHN: My wife hates camping.

PETER: (*Grabs JOHN by the arm.*) John, I'm scared. (*Points to the model.*) This house is our last chance, the last chance to save our marriage, and make our kids understand that we're serious about our future, too. (*Points back to the model.*) It's here, our dream retreat, just at our fingertips and our kids are spinning out of control under our very noses. John, is this going to work? Is this cabin going to be the answer?

JOHN: (*Quietly.*) No.

PETER: I can't hear you.

JOHN: NO! It's not going to be the answer, not even close.

PETER: Don't tell me that. Be a friend, not a naysayer. Lie to me.

JOHN: It won't work. Running away to some idyllic spot in the mountains won't work. Even Thoreau eventually left Walden Pond.

PETER: For what? To return to his life of quiet desperation? Watching everything and everyone going downhill in a hand basket? (*Yells.*) NO! We're building this cabin and I'll put razor wire and search lights around it and mine the road. We are not going to be supporting our adult children until they're forty or raising our grand children. We won't do it! I'll put up guard towers, for God's sake. We will build our dream retreat or die in the attempt.

JOHN: (*Pauses.*) I guess you won't be having a mother-in-law room either?

PETER: No.

JOHN: Aren't your parents in pretty bad physical and psychological shape, too?

PETER: Yes, they are, and getting worse every day. But they've got to go to a nursing home when the time comes. They've got to die peacefully, with dignity. . . .

JOHN: And leave you the money to build your retreat?

PETER: (*Quietly.*) Yes.

JOHN: I didn't hear you.

PETER: YES! They will have to die and leave us the money for the cabin. (*Trails off.*)

JOHN: (*Toys with the model.*) How many solar panels?

PETER: Eighteen, with battery back up for power outages.

JOHN: And is there enough sun up there with all those trees? It's awful rainy and cloudy up there, too. Will you be able to even use the solar panels?

PETER: I hope to God! We've got to. (*Grabs JOHN.*) Pray for sunshine, will you?

JOHN: (*Hugs PETER.*) Of course I will. I'll pray for lots of sunshine.

PETER: Pray for all of us, will you?

JOHN: Of course.

(*Lights dim to dark.*)

THE END

BUILDING A CASH COW

CAST OF CHARACTERS

FRED: Physician project lead. Middle-aged, well dressed. Not in a white coat.

ROBERT (BOBBY): Potential physician investor-partner. Well dressed, perhaps in a suit or sport jacket. Husband of Carlotta.

CARLOTTA (CHARLIE): Robert's wife. A middle-aged woman in ostentatious clothing, lots of flashy jewelry and a designer handbag, perhaps Louis Vuitton, Gucci or Coach.

SETTING

There are minimal set elements. There is a cardboard table with a model of a surgical center on it. It can be made out of foam board, with a few fake little trees, like any real architectural model.

FRED: (*Shows ROBERT the model on the table.*) Look at this beauty! It will have 12 operative suites, a huge clerical area; break rooms, a waiting room with original artwork and electronic announcement boards, all HIPAA compliant, of course.

ROBERT: Very impressive.

FRED: And there's a 200-car, landscaped parking lot with security cameras and ten handicapped parking slots. Everything's handicap accessible, of course, because we're bound to have a lot of those folks all the time.

ROBERT: And an emergency room?

FRED: (*Stares at ROBERT.*) What! Are you crazy?

ROBERT: I mean for emergencies, it's a hospital, isn't it?

FRED: (*Takes ROBERT by the arm.*) Of course it's not a hospital! That's the whole point. This is a for-profit, physician owned and operated investment with no ER.

ROBERT: So where are the acutely ill patients supposed to go?

FRED: To the ER, of course, at the real hospitals. (*Pauses.*) Robert, that's the beauty of it. We take only the elective cases. Maybe an overnight stay at most. They all have insurance and we pocket the profit.

ROBERT: Ah, cherry picking.

FRED: You're damned right! (*Pauses.*) Do you really want to take care of those complicated uninsured patients who pay nothing and turn around and sue you because of a bad outcome? Is that what you want?

ROBERT: No, of course not. I see enough of those folks at the "real" hospitals.

FRED: Exactly! (*Admires the model.*) In this high-tech cash cow, we treat our own well-paying insured patients and leave the Medicaid and uninsured for the hospitals to worry about. That's what they're there for, right?

ROBERT: (*Skeptically.*) Isn't this all too good to be true? And is it even legal?

FRED: No, it's not too good to be true. And yes, it is legal, at least for the time being. There's a lot of talk out there about limiting or eliminating licenses for physician-owned surgery centers. Some bullshit about their negative impact on community hospitals. So we have to act fast! I've already got about 100 physician owner-investors signed up. (*Shows him a contract.*) So it's time for you to sign up and write a deposit check.

ROBERT: This is a big decision and a lot of money. I'll have to ask my wife about it.

FRED: Of course, of course. That's why I invited her to join us down here.

ROBERT: (*Surprised.*) You did?

FRED: Yes, she's a great gal. Everyone loves her. Your wife and my wife are on several charitable boards together. Besides, to get a loan of this magnitude, you'll need her to co-sign anyway.

CARLOTTA: (*Walks in. Swings her brand name purse and flashes her jewelry.*) Am I in the right place?

FRED: You bet! (*Greets CARLOTTA with a friendly kiss.*) You look terrific.

CARLOTTA: (*Goes to ROBERT and kisses him on the cheek.*) Hello, dear. (*Looks at the model.*) So this is the little cash cow you were telling me about.

FRED: (*Laughs.*) No! This is the big cash cow! We expect over 100,000 client visits a year, generating well over 5 million dollars annually in profits after overhead and taxes. Put that in your pipe and smoke it.

CARLOTTA: Smoke it, eh? I'm already high just thinking about it. (*Spins to ROBERT.*) Tuscany, New Zealand, Bali, the Riviera, Aspen, Sedona, Salzburg! (*Clutches ROBERT.*) We can travel the world and leave this miserable place behind.

ROBERT: My dear, I would still have to work. In fact, I would probably be working even more, not less.

CARLOTTA: Yes, of course you would have to work harder. (*To FRED.*) We all have to make sacrifices on the altar of medicine, don't we Freddy? (*Turns back to ROBERT.*) Well, did you sign yet?

ROBERT: Not yet. I'm still concerned that this would damage my relationship with the local hospitals.

CARLOTTA: What! Really, honey, they'd throw you under the bus in a New Orleans minute. You're already been on every hospital committee known to man or God and for what? So they can piss their profits down the rat hole of indigent care?

FRED: (*Applauds.*) Well said! Right on!

ROBERT: The hospitals really don't have a choice about indigent care, Charlie. With EMTALA, they have to treat all emergencies cases, insured or not.

FRED: (*To CARLOTTA.*) I thought your name was Carlotta?

CARLOTTA: (*To FRED.*) Technically it is, but Bobby calls me Charlie, a friendly little nickname from my student years. (*To ROBERT.*) I don't care about EM-TA-LA. I do care about this cash cow!

FRED: Well, Charlie, maybe you can just close this deal for the both of you. Robert will be the one hundredth physician and wife investor. Remember, Bali and Salzburg are waiting. (*Kisses CARLOTTA's hand.*)

CARLOTTA: (*Winks to FRED.*) You little devil, you.

ROBERT: Can I interrupt this love fest and get back to business?

CARLOTTA and FRED: Of course, of course. (*Both laugh.*)

ROBERT: I thought you didn't really know one another?

FRED: (*Backs away from CARLOTTA.*) We have met at social events, the hospital galas, fundraisers and that sort of thing. My wife introduced us.

ROBERT: (*To FRED.*) I thought you were separated or divorced?

FRED: (*Pauses.*) Well, technically I am, but my ex and I remain best friends.

CARLOTTA: (*To ROBERT.*) For heaven's sake, can you let Freddy's personal life out of this? (*Points to the model.*) This is a business discussion, not a social gathering. (*Walks around the model. Bumps into FRED. Giggles.*) I'm sorry. Clumsy me. I get so carried away sometimes.

ROBERT: I have misgivings. National law forbids physician-owned labs because of the dangers of self-referral. How can this be any different? We would be self-referring our own patients?

FRED: It's different because it's not illegal . . .yet.

CARLOTTA: Bobby, sign the damn paper! I certainly will. (*Takes the contract and signs it.*) There! It's done. Someone has got to have the balls in the family. (*Smiles at FRED.*)

ROBERT: (*Crosses his arms.*) I won't do it! I don't care if it costs me money. It's not right, even if it is legal for the time being. Maybe we all ought to share the burden of indigent care? That's the socially responsible thing to do.

FRED: We can't, even if we wanted to. The burden is too great. Half the population in this hellhole has no insurance at all, or just has Medicaid, that doesn't pay shit. You couldn't even run an office on that sort of reimbursement. (*Pauses.*) Do you even take Medicaid patients in your office?

ROBERT: Only when I absolutely have to, and that's pretty rare.

FRED: Exactly! Because you'd go broke and couldn't afford to keep Charlie here livin' in the manner to which she has grown accustomed.

CARLOTTA: Exactly!

ROBERT: (*To CARLOTTA.*) You're in a 10,000 square foot mansion on a lake with marble floors and a walk-in fireplace.

CARLOTTA: Yes! And remember that I open it up for every charitable board to tour every time they want to hold some reception or concert or fundraiser. That house gets more traffic than Grand Central Station. (*To ROBERT.*) I'm the perfect hostess for you in the perfect location and I'm glad to do it. I want everyone to benefit from our prosperity. (*Pauses.*) And there are so many people coming through our home, I don't even know who's coming and going half the time.

ROBERT: I'm sorry. That's true. You're amazingly generous with your time and our home. (*Pauses.*) I just don't feel right about this surgery center deal. There's something dirty and sinister behind the multimillion-dollar façade. How can we build this luxury surgery center and deny it to those hordes that need it the most, just so we can live in a mansion?

FRED: Which you slave day and night to pay for, I might add. We all do. We all sacrifice family, friends, hobbies, health, free time and sleep and God knows what else, just to take care of the sick. And then they still turn around and sue us (*Pauses.*) Why not live in luxury? Why not be able to send our kids to the finest, most expensive schools in the world and not worry about the cost?

CARLOTTA: (*Looking at ROBERT. Quietly.*) So you'd really rather not sign?

ROBERT: Can we think about it a little while?

FRED: NO! You can't. It's now or never! If we let this financing go and miss the application deadline from the regulatory agency, we'll miss our golden opportunity. Robert, you've got to shit or get off the pot! (*To CARLOTTA.*) Can't you give your husband some of your balls? You understand! You know the benefits! Get this little dickless wonder to sign the damn paper, now!

CARLOTTA: (*To FRED. Hits him across the head with her brand-name purse.*) You miserable greedy-ass bully! I can insult my husband, because we love each other. But you can't! (*Throws the contract at FRED.*) Take your contract and shove it up your philandering ass! (*Takes ROBERT by the hand.*) Come on, dear. Maybe I can live without Tuscany or even Bali. (*Sighs.*) But I would at least like to get this really nice looking Mignon Faget necklace and bracelet set down in New Orleans. You know, Mignon's a local Louisiana artist, so we would be supporting the local economy. You would do that for me, wouldn't you? We'd be building social capital, you know.

ROBERT: (*Pauses.*) And you won't hate me forever for not signing on to the golden cash cow?

CARLOTTA: (*Hugs him.*) How could I hate an idealistic dreamer? That's the guy I married, isn't it? (*Pulls ROBERT away.*) Let's go. (*To FRED.*) Sorry Freddy, and by the way, you're a prick and don't call me at the house anymore. Nice people don't call other people's wives at their homes when their husbands aren't there.

FRED and ROBERT: Really?

CARLOTTA: Yes, really! (*Takes ROBERT by the arm.*) Come on Bobby, we need to get you back to the office. Time is money, you know, with or without the cash cow. Don't shirk on your productivity. I still may want to visit Salzburg this winter or maybe the Doctor's Ball at Vienna on New Year's Eve.

(*CARLOTTA and ROBERT walk offstage. FRED is left with the model.*)

FRED: (*Yells. Shakes his fist.*) Fools! You'll regret it! (*Picks up the papers from the floor.*) What a stupid bitch! (*Stands over the model and shakes his head.*)

(*Lights dim to dark.*)

THE END

BUILDING THE TAJ MAHAL

CAST OF CHARACTERS

AMRITA: Middle aged woman. Her ethnicity suggests East Indian, although the dress is not tradition. (Amrita means "full of nectar" in Hindi.)

KAMINI: Middle aged woman. Her ethnicity should be the same as that of AMRITA, whatever the director choses.

SETTING

There is a table and Amrita and Kamini are working on a model of the Taj Mahal as a centerpiece for an undetermined event. There are a couple of chairs that they can sit in from time to time as they work and talk.

AMRITA: My son has decided to marry his girlfriend, Susan.

KAMINI: Susan! The girl he met up in Boston? You must be crushed.

AMRITA: She seems like a nice girl and they love one another, as much as young people of that age can. Susan graduated from SUNY.

KAMINI: SUNY? Isn't that a second rate state school up there in New York somewhere?

AMRITA: Yes, it's in New York and I think she graduated from the film program. Sound design, I think. From what Susan says, it's an excellent program, one of the best in the country.

KAMINI: Hmmm. He must really love her to marry down like that.

AMRITA: Down?

KAMINI: Well, yes. Your son's got a master's degree, a professional degree from Harvard and she's from some cheap public school.

AMRITA: Cheap, I really don't know. But SUNY's not an expensive Ivy League school for sure. (*Pauses.*) And your daughter? You must be disappointed for her as well.

KAMINI: What on earth for?

AMRITA: Marrying some old schnook from Detroit. Doesn't sound too nice to me.

KAMINI: That old schnook, as you call him, is worth several million. He owns a string of retail stores across the city. They live in a home on the upper side, which is still very nice, and their home must be worth two million or more, even in that area's depressed real estate market.

AMRITA: Very impressive, but does she love him?

KAMINI: Of course she loves him. Why shouldn't she?

AMRITA: Because he's twice her age, has been previously married with several grown children, and he's very dark-skinned.

KAMINI: Amrita! I'm ashamed of you. That is a very unkind thing of you to say.

AMRITA: Which part? Being old? Previously married? Or just too dark-skinned?

KAMINI: All three! You'd think we were still in the Old World arranging these things from afar like our parents did.

AMRITA: And that's not what happened? You're telling me you had nothing to do with negotiating your daughter's marriage with the help of a few mutual friends and busybody relatives here and abroad?

KAMINI: Perhaps we helped a little bit. (*Pauses.*) But they really do love one another.

AMRITA: So do Susan and my son.

KAMINI: But a sound technician? Really?

AMRITA: Yes, it's odd, but it might work out. They'll be leaving for Uganda right after the marriage.

KAMINI: Uganda? How could you let them go to such a god-forsaken, dangerous place like that?

AMRITA: They're adults, Kamini, what can you do? (*Puts a piece if the model in place.*) Besides, didn't you come to this poor depressed rural part of America with your husband? Didn't we both?

KAMINI: America is not Uganda. We came to seek opportunity and make our fortune. And we have done both. (*Pauses.*) By the way, what kind of a family does your son's fiancée come from? At least she's (*pauses*) like us, isn't she?

AMRITA: No, she's not exactly "like us." Her family is from some little island in the South Pacific, some deserted atoll. Besides, her parents are already dead.

KAMINI: An orphan as well. That's sad. (*Pauses.*) I remember sailing through those islands on the way to America as a child. We had been expulsed from Tanzania by the new local dictator and we sailed through those tropical islands, squalid villages next to crystal clear lagoons.

It was like having a slum in a tropical paradise. (*Pauses.*) Is there any chance they may call the marriage off?

AMRITA: I don't think so. They're eloping anyway, doing a civil ceremony with a couple of witnesses and us.

KAMINI: No priests? No music? No lavish reception?

AMRITA: No, nothing. Their choice.

KAMINI: (*Pauses.*) I must say that when my husband and I got married, we had a simple ceremony.

AMRITA: (*Ironically.*) What! No priests, no music and no reception?

KAMINI: No, it was shameful, but we were poor at that time. We only had our intellects, our dreams and our determination. In fact, my husband was clutching onto his diploma, wrapped in a Ziploc bag with other important papers. It was degrading and humiliating, but it couldn't be helped. His family had been expulsed, just like ours, but from another nasty little country by another nasty little racist dictator.

AMRITA: (*Takes KAMINI by the shoulders.*) Look how far you've come! A huge house, three wonderful children in terrific Eastern schools, your husband with a wonderful job and a very impressive salary. You must be very proud and very happy.

KAMINI: (*Slowly, without conviction.*) Yes, proud and happy. (*Sighs. Pauses.*) No, proud and unhappy. My husband works day and night. He never sees me and when he does, he looks at me like I'm one of his employees. He doesn't even touch me anymore. (*Pauses.*) I think he might be having an affair, but I'm not sure.

AMRITA: I'm so sorry. But your children, they are both so successful and happy!

KAMINI: Yes, successful and happy and very far away. (*Pauses.*) They live thousands of miles away where they can get good jobs commensurate with their fine educations. Neither of them have children because they are too busy with their work and their careers. So they are there and I am here, isolated, rich and miserable. (*Pauses.*) I feel like some wealthy freak, unloved at home and in the community. It's terrible.

AMRITA: Your children come home from time to time. And you visit them as well, don't you?

KAMINI: Yes, but it's not like you. You and your children seem so happy, so normal, so fulfilled. (*Gestures.*) Look at your home, this workshop. You help in the community and have friends and serve on all sorts of charitable and artistic boards.

AMRITA: You could, too. You just need to start donating your time and money.

KAMINI: What! And waste our hard-earned money on these silly groups that only want us to help them out by paying them something.

AMRITA: So? That's they way it works. We all need to give.

KAMINI: We do give, to a host of parasitic relatives scattered all over the United States and the world. I tell my husband it's exploitation, but he says it's for the advancement of the family. Yes, he gives to the family half way round the world and doesn't even have a caress to spare for me at night. Everything for the family around the world, but no tenderness for me at home in bed. (*Angrily.*) What kind of love is that, anyway?

AMRITA: Do you love him?

KAMINI: I don't know anymore. (*Pauses.*) I didn't even know him when we got married. It was one of those traditional things, of course. (*Pauses.*) I think I admired and respected him more than I loved him.

(*Pauses.*) I thought that love would follow like my mother told me it would.

AMRITA: It did work out that way with my husband. We didn't know one another either before our marriage, but we fell in love and stayed in love, best friends and lovers.

KAMINI: Not with me. (*Pauses.*) It just stopped with respect, and then went into raising children and getting them in the best schools and the best professions. Doctor or engineer was their only choice. My second son wanted to go into creative writing. Can you believe that?

AMRITA: Sure. Why not, if it brings him happiness.

KAMINI: Yes, sure, the happiness of starving in the street, or worse yet, becoming some parasitic emasculated creature still living at home at forty. It's appalling.

AMRITA: My second son thought about it, but went into public health. He's in Nepal now, I think. Or maybe it's Myanmar? He said he could always make a living, but he wanted to make a difference.

KAMINI: (*Pauses.*) How odd.

AMRITA: He seems happy and never asks for money.

KAMINI: Money, money and more money. It flows in and flows out. Another house, another diploma, another course of study, an unexpected family expense. It never seems to end. (*Pauses.*) Except in death.

AMRITA: Like with Dr. Bandhu.

KAMINI: Yes, like him. He just died and no one ever gives him a second thought. There he was in his coffin, surrounded by successful out-of-town children, who all owned businesses, offices, clinics, industries, hotel franchises. He looked so small, so lonely, almost like an afterthought in someone else's party, like a vase of flowers or a particularly beautiful ice sculpture that melts away during the evening or this Taj Mahal centerpiece. (*Points to the model.*)

AMRITA: Dr. Bandhu was revered in the community, at least among our people.

KAMINI: Yes, our people. (*Thoughtfully.*) I heard he wanted his ashes placed in the river near where he was born, a half a world away.

AMRITA: That's nice. But I want to be cremated and have my ashes strewn in a public garden here in town, if they allow such a thing here.

KAMINI: What? And not in a columbarium in a place of honor?

AMRITA: No! In a hundred years, who will know who I was? Who will care? But if I bloom as a rose in the spring, just one perfect blossom, then perhaps some random passerby will look at me and smile. Or maybe he or she will bend down and smell the hint of a fragrance on some dewy morning. (*Mimics smelling a rose.*)

KAMINI: That's lovely, Amrita, really lovely. (*Pauses and considers the proposition.*) No, flower gardens stink! The public garden here is filled with trash and smells like dog poop. (*Pauses.*) It's tempting to be rosebud, but I really do want a monument, one so large and intricate that no passerby can help but stop and admire it, something wonderful and grandiose.

AMRITA: (*Indicates the building.*) Like the Taj Mahal?

KAMINI: Yes, precisely. Like the Taj Mahal. (*Points to the model.*) People flock to that place. It's crawling with tourists who are all told about the undying love of the sultan for his deceased wife. Yes, she's still remembered all these many centuries later. That's what I want, too.

AMRITA: (*Pauses.*) And maybe it will be so with you, too. Who knows?

KAMINI: (*Places the finishing touches on the center piece.*) I can only hope.

AMRITA: It's beautiful, the perfect centerpiece, much better than Mr. Bandhu's corpse. Don't' you think?

KAMINI: Yes, certainly and something to remember us by after the reception.

AMRITA: Maybe, if only for few minutes. That would be nice, too, and maybe the best anyone can hope for.

(*AMRITA takes KAMINI by the hand. Lights dim to dark.*)

THE END

BUILDING A CHATEAU
IN HESSMER

CAST OF CHARACTERS

CHARLES: A middle-aged man. Very self-satisfied. Dressed in casual chic.

DILETTE: Charles's middle aged wife. Down to earth. More frumpy in appearance and perhaps with a mild French-Louisiana Southern accent.

SETTING

Charles and Dilette are standing near a model (or picture) of a very large and imposing house on a card table. It is an architectural model (if a photo is not used.) There are a couple of chairs they can sit in from time to time.

CHARLES: Isn't it a beauty?

DILETTE: (Sitting *down. Knitting or doing embroidery. Looks up briefly.*) Yes, it's a very nice looking house.

CHARLES: Very nice? (*Looks back at the model.*) It's a one-of-a-kind 10,000 square foot mansion, patterned after a château in the Loire Valley in France. It's a castle, a château, not a house.

DILETTE: Yes, it's certainly a castle, but in Hessmer, Louisiana?

CHARLES: You better believe it! (*Admires the model. Turns it slightly.*) The walls will be made of brick over cinderblock. I talked to the architect about using imported limestone, but that was even too expensive for me. (*Pauses.*) There will be 14-foot ceilings downstairs and 12-foot ceilings upstairs, with Bohemian glass chandeliers and Italian marble floors and counters, and a 40-person dining room table, walk-in closets and pantries galore. It'll be swell, Dilette, you'll see.

DILETTE: Can we afford this?

CHARLES: Of course we can afford this! (*Spins around.*) The money keeps flowing in from all directions. It's manna from heaven. It's amazing the judgments from class action suits, big oil, big trucks, malpractice, car wrecks, and more and more. It's unbelievable, even to me. There's so much money to be made and I'm making it as fast as I can.

DILETTE: A château in Hessmer? (*Points to the model.*) Do we really need something like this?

CHARLES: Need it? We don't need it. I want it! I want every loser for a hundred miles around to know that I'm rich and I'll make them rich, too, if I can get their case.

DILETTE: Isn't that what all your billboards are for?

CHARLES: Those things? They're part of a larger strategy to get my face out there, and also something to irritate and frighten my competitors. Television, radio, billboards, the Internet, it's all just to make my name known to every potential litigant in this parish and in the whole state. There's almost no one who doesn't know my name and my face now. This house is only going to help spread the glory of my mission and my name.

DILETTE: Your name?

CHARLES: (*Looks bewildered and then speaks.*) Our name, of course. We're married and happily so, I might add.

DILETTE: My parents lived in a 2-bedroom shack with wooden floors and no air-conditioning.

CHARLES: Mine, too. But that's not what we have now, and that's not what our kids will have, either. They'll live in a château, a real one.

They'll go to the best, most expensive private schools in the country and marry into old money families like the Howards or the Hirondelles.

DILETTE: Why?

CHARLES: So we can be part of the landed gentry, too, the old money of the state that always sends their kids to Eastern Ivy League schools and who sit on corporate boards and start big charitable foundations.

DILETTE: We're from the East, too.

CHARLES: (*Laughs derisively.*) Yeah, Eastern Avoyelles Parish!

DILETTE: And what's wrong with that? Your family and my family, both came to Louisiana as penniless French immigrants and bought their land, that's still in the family. That makes us landed gentry, too, doesn't it?

CHARLES: (*Laughs.*) You gotta be kidding. What are a few acres along *Bayou des Glaises* compared to owning hundreds of thousands of acres scattered across the whole center of the state, and all the trees covering it and all the oil and gas under it. That's landed gentry. That's real wealth, real generational wealth.

DILETTE: We have real wealth, too.

CHARLES: Yes, finally. And look at us now! We could buy all of Hessmer and Cottonport and Mansura and have a lot left over, too.

DILETTE: Who would want it? Who would want to buy Mansura? Where would the people go? I don't want to own Mansura. I'd rather go out and eat *cochon-de-lait* and cracklings at the festival and listen to the music and watch the people on the carnival rides.

CHARLES: Dilette, Chèrie, you can eat caviar on toast while you sip *Veuve Cliquot* champagne, not Abita Beer. Forget the cracklings. Forget your humble roots. Move up the social ladder let's take our place in the sun, thanks to big oil, big trucks and big hospitals. (*Grabs DILETTE. Spins her around in a waltz step.*) We can two-step to *valses musettes* in Paris instead of Mansura. The sky's the limit and we need to let everyone know we have made it into the big time. That's what building this château is all about.

DILETTE: So everyone can hate us? So the Hirondelles and the Howards can look down their noses at us because we're the "*nou-veau riche.*" (*Pauses.*) If the poor people hate us because we're rich and the rich people disdain us because we're just the newly wealthy, where would we be exactly?

CHARLES: We'd be in the biggest, grandest, damnedest house in this parish, that's where we'll be.

DILETTE: And when our children move away because they've been educated in fancy Eastern schools with other children from rich families, will they come back to Avoyelles Parish? Will they?

CHARLES: Why would we care? We can fly anywhere in the world, anytime we want. Let our kids live in New York, or Boston, or Paris. Who cares where they want to live. We can visit them there.

DILLETTE: I care! (*Pauses.*) I care because they'll grow up and have children and I will not be there to put a bandage on their skinned knees, or cradle them in my arms when the thunder rolls, or make them chocolate chip cookies when they come home from school.

CHARLES: School! Like that dump where you went to school and where the kids graduate without ever learning to read or write?

DILETTE: You went there, too! Yes, and by the grace of God, I got a good education. And so did you. There were some wonderful, dedicated teachers.

CHARLES: Let's not talk about the school. Forget the past. (*Takes DILETTE in his arms.*) Think about owning a condo at Aspen, a beach house in Pensacola, and maybe a little place in London or Paris. You can meet your grandchildren and feed then chocolate éclairs instead of chocolate chip cookies.

DILETTE: (*Starts to cry.*) I don't want it! I don't want this château or the condos or seeing my grandchildren for a few days in Europe. (*Pauses.*) What happened to the guy who thought a day off at Spring Bayou was a real treat? What happened to him?

CHARLES: He's dead and gone and good riddance.

DILLETTE: Killed by money! Killed by greed! Killed by big oil, big rigs and big hospitals while you thought you were getting the best of them all.

CHARLES: I'm helping my clients and they're very grateful.

DILETTE: You're helping yourself. The clients are a pitiful afterthought, a means to an end. I hate you! I hate what you've become!

CHARLES: (*Angrily.*) Then go! Go back to your miserable little house in Cottonport, your creepy little hovel filled with cheap furniture and old hand-me-downs.

DILETTE: And love. Don't' forget the love. Don't forget my parents and siblings who took you in like a son and a brother when your own family kicked you out. (*Points to the model.*) This is not a house, it's a mausoleum and I'm not dead yet.

CHARLES: (*Pauses.*) Yes you are. You're dead to me.

DILETTE: (*Tries to embrace him.*) Charles, no!

CHARLES: (*Points off stage.*) Get out! Get out and don't come back. If I can bring down big oil, I can figure out how to get a divorce.

DILETTE: I can find a lawyer, too. You'll lose half of everything you own.

CHARLES: It would be worth it to get rid of a country clown like you. You're a dead weight that drags me down and I need to soar with the eagles, not wallow with the pigs.

DILETTE: Pigs! I thought I was an anchor, something that held you to the earth, something that keeps you from sailing away and never coming back, some stability in your crazy life.

CHARLES: Stability! Hell no! You are an albatross around my neck that is suffocating me. Your petty provincial thoughts, your country accent that spews out every time you open your mouth. Those ridiculous rags you wear when you could dress like a duchess. It's pathetic. You're pathetic!

DILETTE: I'm sorry you don't like the way I dress or the way I talk. I'm sorry it has to end like this. I'm leaving. (*Picks up her knitting.*)

CHARLES: Go! (*Turns his back.*) There are a hundred women in this God-forsaken parish that would give their right boob to be where you're standing.

DILETTE: (*Laughs.*) Good! You go ahead and surround yourself with a hundred one-breasted, gold-digging hussies. That ought to be good for a laugh. (*Laughs again.*)

CHARLES: (*Turns around.*) Don't you dare laugh at me! No one laughs at me!

DILETTE: Why not? You're ridiculous, just like a château in Hessmer. (*Laughs and knocks the model off the table.*)

CHARLES: Shut up! (*Slaps DILETTE.*)

DILETTE: (*Looks shocked. Touches her face.*) I'm leaving now. Enjoy your new home and your new life and your new so-called friends. Maybe the Howards and Hirondelles will learn to like you one day, but I doubt it. They will hold you in contempt and you'll deserve it. (*Exits.*)

CHARLES: (*Watches DILETTE leave. Looks back at the model, not at DILETTE leaving. Picks up the model and puts it back on the table.*) Slate. I want real slate on the roof. None of those fake tiles. And I want faucets made out of solid 24 karat gold. And when Noël comes, I want so many lights that you can see the house a mile away or more. (*Sits down.*) And a *porte cochère* and a wine cellar, and my portrait in the entrance. I want a life-size royal portrait by a famous artist, maybe with a Blue Dog or something like that. I want it six feet tall and right in the front so when people come in, no one could possibly miss it. (*Stands up and gestures around.*) I can see it now. It will be beautiful, *magnifique*! *Complètement magnifique*! (*Lights dim to dark.*)

THE END

A BELGIAN QUARTET

A BELGIAN WAKE

DINING AT AUDERGHEM

COFFEE AT LOLA'S

AN EVENING IN PERUWELZ

A BELGIAN WAKE

CAST OF CHARACTERS

BEATRICE: An older woman conservatively dressed and with correct speech. Perhaps a hint of a foreign accent, French or British.

MARGARET: A middle-aged woman, dressed in conservative, dark clothing. No regional accent.

SETTING

There is a table and they are drinking coffee and eating pieces of open-faced fruit tarts.

BEATRICE: It was a "mouroir," an antechamber to death, that's all.

MARGARET: That's insulting! Nadine got as good a care as she could have hoped for under the circumstances.

BEATRICE: What! In that cold, dirty, under-staffed nursing home in the middle of nowhere? How can you say she got good care? It's incredible.

MARGARET: Because she didn't have any money left! (*Pauses.*) There were no other options. She couldn't afford to go back to the capital. It would have cost the double and the care wouldn't have been any better, just more expensive.

BEATRICE: You say that because you wanted to get whatever was left over from Nadine's estate, that's all.

MARGARET: That's a lie! There's nothing left in her estate. And you're saying what you do because you didn't get the house and contents like she said you would so many years ago.

BEATRICE: No, I didn't get them, did I? Some local money-grubbing nurse got them. That's a real deal for her. The nurse gets the house. Now that's an ethical violation if I've ever heard one. And you get the leftovers and her other devoted friends get the shaft. (*Pauses.*) I cared about her. I wasn't family, but neither were you.

MARGARET: Her niece in America is coming to the funeral, believe it or not.

BEATRICE: (*Surprised.*) Really? What for?

MARGARET: Because she is the only surviving blood relative.

BEATRICE: Well, she should have taken better care of Nadine instead of delegating it to someone like you here in Belgium. You don't even live in this country.

MARGARET: Taken care of her from America? How was Nadine's niece supposed to have done that?

BEATRICE: She could have done a better job than you did from England, that's for sure.

MARGARET: Can you just shut up? You come barreling in here for the funeral full of spite and spew it all around over everyone.

BEATRICE: Everyone? No, just you, because you had power of attorney, which you abused in my humble opinion!

MARGARET: First, there is nothing humble about you! Second, Nadine chose me for power of attorney and I did not abuse her or her finances. That was a court decision and she agreed.

BEATRICE: The court! Yes, precipitated by you so you could salvage something of the estate. It's abusive.

43

MARGARET: Abusive? No, but what was certainly abusive was the gardener who charged double, and delivery man who took a huge tip with each delivery, and a housekeeper who benefited from sums of money that mysteriously disappeared from the house. That's abusive! (Pauses.) A lonely woman living in the country, surrounded by unscrupulous peasants. That's abuse. There's nothing left, nothing at all.

BEATRICE: All that really happened?

MARGARET: Yes, that and more.

BEATRICE: What more?

MARGARET: Someone broke into her home and tore it apart, looking for hidden money and jewelry. I suppose.

BEATRICE: (*Surprised.*) When did that happen?

MARGARET: Just a couple of weeks ago. And when they didn't find anything, they tore the place up and pissed on the carpets, and all that just a few weeks before she died. That's abuse.

BEATRICE: Did they find the criminals?

MARGARET: Of course not. (*Pauses.*) So who's being abusive? Who's the criminal?

BEATRICE: I'm angry, that's all.

MARGARET: And guilty?

BEATRICE: No, of course not!

MARGARET: Not even a little because you weren't here either to do everything you could for a dear old friend?

BEATRICE: I did do everything I could, and more!

MARGARET: Really? (*Pauses.*) Couldn't you have called more often? Or adopted her little dog that she had to give away to the housekeeper? Or been more attentive on the holidays since you were so much closer than I was?

BEATRICE: That's ridiculous.

MARGARET: Really? Is it so ridiculous as that? (*Pauses.*) Maybe some of that anger is mis-directed guilt?

BEATRICE: (*Pauses.*) Maybe.

MARGARET: How do you think it feels, living in another country and coming from time to time while knowing that Nadine was a so alone? How did you think I felt only being able to call every week and say hello? Her niece from America did as much, calling twice a week for years.

BEATRICE: How did you feel?

MARGARET: I felt sick with guilt. But I couldn't do any more and I refused to translate my guilt into anger. What good would it do? Yelling at the nursing home staff? Would that have gotten Nadine better care? (*Pauses.*) I think not. What do you think?

BEATRICE: (*Pauses.*) Probably not, but it might have made you feel better.

MARGARET: Do you really think so? Do you really feel better now that you've insulted me and the care I gave to Nadine?

BEATRICE: No, I don't. I feel ashamed, ashamed of myself, ashamed of this miserable little town, and ashamed of you.

MARGARET: (*Pauses.*) Don't you think we ought to bury our resentments with Nadine? What good will resentment do? What do you say? Give me a hug!

BEATRICE: (*Reluctantly hugs MARGARET.*) Okay.

MARGARET: (*Takes a bottle of brandy and pours out two glasses.*) Nadine wanted us to have some brandy at the wake. (*Hands a glass to BEATRICE.*) Here's to Nadine, a friend to both of us!

BEATRICE: To Nadine! (*Drinks.*)

MARGARET: By the way, what to you think of the tombstone?

BEATRICE: Very beautiful. I liked the bronze doves flying up from the top.

MARGARET: It cost her a pretty penny, too, all paid for in advance, plus fifty years of perpetual care.

BEATRICE: Isn't her brother there in the vault, too?

MARGARET: Well, actually it's her cousin, not her brother, but they were raised like siblings. And yes, he's right underneath. (*Leans closer to BEATRICE.*) Nadine told me that she and her cousin had had a great discussion about their burial during one of his visits here. They downed a bottle of fine Bordeaux and argued on and on about who was going to be on top for eternity. (*Pauses.*) She won, of course.

BEATRICE: Won?

MARGARET: Yes, he died years ago, so she's on top.

BEATRICE: Well, at least for the next fifty years. After that, who knows? They'll dug them both up and incinerate the remains and put someone else there. That's how it works around here, isn't it?

MARGARET: After fifty years, who cares? We'll be gone, and her niece in America, too, and all the rest of her friends and relatives. (*Raises her brandy.*) To Nadine! May she rest in peace!

BEATRICE: To Nadine, our friend and colleague!

(*BEATRICE and MARGARET down their glasses. Lights dim to dark.*)

THE END

DINING IN AUDERGHEM

49

CAST OF CHARACTERS

PIERRE: Older gentleman, casually dressed. Somewhat imperious in style and speech.

CATHERINE: Pierre's wife. Quiet, soft-spoken, takes care of the table.

DANIEL: Middle-aged, casually dressed.

NANETTE: Daniel's wife. Tall, slender, with a natural elegance.

SETTING

The couples are around a dinner table discussing. The table setting is modern, uncluttered.

PIERRE: No, I would not do it again!

DANIEL: Why?

PIERRE: Twenty years ago, I wanted to show cultural fraternity among all Belgians. We recorded as many folk songs in French as in Flemish. It was an expression of Belgian solidarity. Now it's finished!

DANIEL: Why?

PIERRE: Because they're taking over, that's why. The Flemish are taking over Brussels one job at a time, one house at a time, one commune at a time. All the jobs in Brussels are for bilingual French-Flemish speakers. And who is bilingual? (*Pauses.*) Just the Flemish, of course! They learn French and English as second languages. They already speak Flemish, so they are the only ones who are perfectly bilingual. Who else could be? So one job at a time, they have invaded the civil service in Brussels. Voilà! *Le fait accompli*. A perfect slow motion takeover.

DANIEL: You are bilingual, too, aren't you?

PIERRE: Yes, of course, but not perfectly. I can manage, especially after practice. But Brussels is a French-speaking city, stuck in the middle of historically Flemish territory. They'll never give up. They'll never let it go. They'll work and scheme and legislate until Brussels is once again a Flemish city in Flanders, and then they'll split the country in two, a rich Flanders and a bankrupt Wallonia.

DANIEL: Sound's a bit like the Jews and Jerusalem, no? It was their historical homeland. And with persistence and force, Jerusalem is part of Israel, too. (*Pause.*) But why can the Flemish get away with it? Why can they exert this sort of pressure?

PIERRE: Why can anyone do anything? (*Pauses.*) Money and power, of course! They have Zeebruge and Zaventem and that entire infrastructure that was built at the expense of the industry in Wallonia, and now what do we have there? Closed factories, closed mines, unemployment and tourism that only the Dutch and Flemish can afford.

DANIEL: Well, tourism is something, isn't it?

(*CATHERINE serves the table in silence.*)

PIERRE: Yes, as long as they leave their money here and disappear. But they're buying up every little farm and country home in Wallonia as their summer residences, investment properties and tax shelters.

DANIEL: (*Looks at his plate. To CATHERINE.*) This looks wonderful. What is it?

CATHERINE: Waterzoi, a typical Belgian dish with a Flemish name.

DANIEL: Thank you so much. (*Tastes the meal.*) It's delicious. (*Turns to NANETTE.*) And what do you think of all this. You're Belgian, too.

NANETTE: Oh, no! I'm American now, and glad of it. I don't want to be in the middle of this conflict. I studied Dutch for 12 years and I can't even speak a full sentence. I wouldn't stand a chance here anymore.

PIERRE: You see! And yet you learned to speak English just fine in America.

DANIEL: With a charming little accent, of course.

NANETTE: No, with a BIG accent. Every time I answer the phone with an "allo," the person says, "Oh, sorry, I must have the wrong number." (*Pauses.*) I am glad to be out of all this ethnic bickering and fighting and horrible city traffic in Brussels. My God, I've been dead with fear every since we got her. I don't know how anyone can drive around here.

CATHERINE: (*Serves more food.*) It takes an hour and a half just to cross the city. It is discouraging.

DANIEL: No wonder you prefer to spend your time in your home in the Ardennes. (*Pauses.*) You do still go there, don't you?

PIERRE: All of our free weekends, plus at least two months in the summertime. We used to travel around to other places in Europe more often, but with the upkeep and renovations and the usually cleaning at the cabin, it seems we spend more and more time there. I'm not sure if we own it or it owns us.

DANIEL: Are your daughters interesting in owning it one day?

PIERRE: They love to drop in for a weekend, but the upkeep? And the taxes? And the distance from Brussels? How could they do all that?

Sure, they like to go there from time to time, but owning it, I think not. (*Pauses.*) When the time comes, I suppose we'll sell it.

DANIEL: To whom?

PIERRE: Ah, good questions. The only ones with the money are the Flemish. First they take over Brussels, then Wallonia. They'll own all of Belgium one of these days.

CATHERINE: More *tarte au sucre*?

DANIEL: No, thank you. It was delicious.

CATHERINE: And you, Nanette?

NANETTE: No, thanks. (*To CATHERINE.*) And how is your work with your father's library going?

CATHERINE: He had over 5,000 books; many of them signed first editions and many gifts from the authors.

NANETTE: They must be of some interest to academics and archivists.

CATHERINE: You would think so. But the archivists only want the correspondence, not the books, and there are thousands of letters from distinguished authors and publishers. It's really extraordinary, but not of much interest to anyone, at least not until they are all sorted and classified. And that takes weeks and weeks.

NANETTE: At least you enjoy the work of sorting through the material, don't you?

CATHERINE: Yes, yes, of course, it's profoundly interesting. I had no idea my father was so important in the world of Spanish letters.

He translated most of the notable contemporary Spanish and Latin American poets in his time. The list just goes on and on.

PIERRE: All swept away with time, like all of us will be. What will remain of this? (*Swings his arms around the room.*) Nothing. Absolutely nothing.

NANETTE: That's cynical.

PIERRE: Not cynical, just realistic.

CATHERINE: Coffee anyone.

PIERRE, DANIEL and NANETTE: Yes, please.

CATHERINE: (*Serves the others.*) I think it's the beauty we create and the kindness we show to one another that somehow lives on after us.

PIERRE: Rubbish!

DANIEL: No, I think Catherine's right. You have shown us kindness and extended friendship that has lasted for decades. It has stood the test of time, at least in our lifetime.

PIERRE: But history, humanity? What of that? Perhaps religious believers have such fantasies, but realistic men and women of science? How can you believe such fairy tales? Perhaps a few of our musical performances, at least those on CDs, may survive as curiosities somewhere, somehow. Perhaps Daniel's books will gain some local notoriety. (*To CATHERINE.*) Like your father's. (*To NANETTE.*) Or perhaps your beautiful eggs, your pysanky, will stand the test of time, as fragile as they are. (*Pauses.*) But I doubt it.

NANETTE: They say pysanky made three thousand years ago are still found as colored shell fragments in ancient tombs, older than Christianity itself.

PIERRE: (*Looks skeptical.*) Perhaps you're right. (*Takes his glass.*) In any case, let's profit from the moment and leave the subject of tombs behind. (*Raises his glass.*) To friendships that withstand the ravages of time and distance!

ALL: To friendship!

(*Lights dim to dark.*)

THE END

COFFEE AT LOLA'S

CAST OF CHARACTERS

ADRIENNE: Older woman with greying hair. Dressed in grey and black. A smoker.

NANETTE: Middle-aged woman, dyed hair. Casually, but stylishly dressed.

SETTING

Café in Brussels. They are seated at a small table outside where Adrienne can smoke.

ADRIENNE: It's my choice. It's my body. I have the right to choose what I do with my own body.

NANETTE: Yes, of course. But smoking is killing you.

ADRIENNE: Yes, even if it's killing me, I have the choice to decide.

NANETTE: That's incredibly egotistical and selfish.

ADRIENNE: No, it's not. It's personal.

NANETTE: True, if it was only you. But you have children and grandchildren who care about you. How would they feel if you died? Wouldn't they be sad?

ADRIENNE: Perhaps they would, but I've already done everything I needed and wanted to do on this earth. I got a good education, I worked for 35 years, I raised a family, and now it doesn't matter if I stay on this earth or not.

NANETTE: You sound depressed.

ADRIENNE: I do feel sad sometimes. But mostly I feel abandoned.

NANETTE: By who?

ADRIENNE: By my father, by my husband and by my children.

NANETTE: Your father was different. He died because he was in the resistance and was Jewish and was shot by the Germans, not because he didn't love you and chose to leave you.

ADRIENNE: True. But to a child, it's the same. And with Frankie, it was different. He left me for another woman. There's no way to fill that void, not even if I wanted to.

NANETTE: He's gone. He's out of your life and has been gone for a decade. You still have your children and grandchildren.

ADRIENNE: Yes, in Israel! What good does that do for me? Seeing them a couple of times a year and talking to them on the phone, even if we do Skype. It's not the same.

NANETTE: Our children don't even do that much. You can still become more involved here in this community. You work with abused children, you volunteer your time. You make a difference in children's lives. (*Pauses.*) And you also kill yourself with cigarettes. It's crazy.

ADRIENNE: Yes, and I'm not likely to stop anytime soon.

NANETTE: As I said, it's selfish and egotistical! You die and your children and grandchildren are deprived of their mother and grandmother. You're just perpetuating the cycle of abandonment. This time, you'd be abandoning them, just like you said your were abandoned. You are a victim, too, but not of your family, of the tobacco industry. Your family cares about you, but Big Tobacco doesn't care about you or your personal problems or even the fact that you'll die young. They want your money and for you to be hooked on cigarettes and that's all they care about. (*Pauses.*) I care about you as a friend. (*Reaches out and touches ADRIENNE's hand.*)

ADRIENNE: And what will this individual psychotherapy session cost me?

NANETTE: Nothing! You have paid a thousand times over by being a friend who listened to my problems over the years.

ADRIENNE: What problems? You have a prosperous and loyal husband, a big house, a rich social life, everything a woman could want.

NANETTE: Our children are scattered all around the U.S. and the world. We don't hear from them for weeks or months at a time. My husband shines so brightly, he eclipses everything and everyone around him, especially me. Does that sound so easy to you?

ADRIENNE: He's still with you, isn't he? That's something.

NANETTE: Yes, physically, but sometimes I think he looks at me like I'm some sort of weight that drags him down.

ADRIENNE: He says that?

NANETTE: No, never! He says things like "You're the love of my life, my reason to get up in the morning, my inspiration, and my source of stability." That's what he says.

ADRIENNE: Well? What's wrong with that?

NANETTE: Nothing, of course. And yet it all seems slightly unreal, somehow like a show, another performance with the world and me as his audience. We're terribly close, yet strangely distant.

ADRIENNE: Maybe you want too much?

NANETTE: Perhaps.

ADRIENNE: Maybe you're just naturally anxious?

NANETTE: It's funny, Daniel always says that a man's greatest fear is emasculation and a woman's greatest fear is abandonment.

ADRIENNE: Well, my fears were realized. How about yours?

NANETTE: Maybe Daniel and I never really connected. Maybe we always lived and interacted on some superficial plain that wasn't even love, but something more like convenience.

ADRIENNE: That's ridiculous.

NANETTE: The night before we got married, I asked him if he wanted to get married. And you know what he answered?

ADRIENNE: (*Shakes her head.*) No, what did he say?

NANETTE: He said "no." He really didn't want to get married. (*Pauses.*) And I couldn't sleep a wink all night. I just stared at the ceiling and wondered if I weren't making the worst mistake of my life.

ADRIENNE: And now, thirty-seven years and four children and several grandchildren later?

NANETTE: I still sometimes wonder.

ADRIENNE: Not wanting to get married and not loving you are two different things. What does he say to that question now? Does he ever say he loves you?

NANETTE: I never ask.

ADRIENNE: Afraid of the answer?

NANETTE: No, not really. (*Pauses.*) We've stopped having sexually relations for almost a couple of years now.

ADRIENNE: That's how it started with me and Frankie. That's more of a problem than not saying he loves you. Frankie said that he just didn't want sex anymore, while he was screwing a female colleague at work.

NANETTE: It's not that. (*Pauses.*) I think he's impotent.

ADRIENNE: You should be over-joyed. I found my conjugal duty to be a burden for years. That's probably why Frankie left me. It's hard to fake that, you know. I got to the point I was more interested in the cigarette afterwards than the act itself. That's a bad sign.

NANETTE: Smoking, smoking, smoking. Why don't you try e-cigarettes instead?

ADRIENNE: There's not too much known about them yet. They might be worse than regular cigarettes for all anyone knows.

NANETTE: They can't be as bad. And you'll get the nicotine, the sensation of holding something, the satisfaction of the vapor cloud, and the feeling of stuffing something into your mouth. (*Pauses.*) Go for it. Go e-cigarette.

ADRIENNE: I don't' know. I don't want to jump from the frying pan into the fire.

NANETTE: You're already in hell, so you might just be able to reach purgatory instead.

ADRIENNE: You and your Catholic notions. Jews don't believe in all that. You Catholics just love your guilt.

NANETTE: And atonement? And forgiveness of sins? And all that, too.

ADRIENNE: Stop! I'll discuss cigarettes and sex, but not religion or politics. (*Raises her glass.*) To a friendship that has survived the stresses and strains of time and distance.

NANETTE: To friendship!

(*Lights dim to dark.*)

THE END

AN EVENING IN PERUWELZ

CAST OF CHARACTERS

THIERRY: Young man with a French style scarf and Gallic affectations.

NANETTE: Thierry's mother. Older, but still young-looking woman. Strong-willed with a foreign accent when she speaks in English.

DANIEL: Nanette's husband and Thierry's father. A middle-aged man in good shape, casually dressed and speaking without an accent.

SETTING

Den or living room. The group is sharing beer or wine and some snack food.

DANIEL: (*To THIERRY.*) Man of mystery! I don't want mysteries; I want answers, real answers.

THIERRY: You'll get answers in good time.

DANIEL: What sort of sadistic behavior is this, anyway? You change your job, you talk like you're separating from your wife, you still live in your mother-in-law's home. You give a mountain of innuendos and not a molehill of facts. What's the big deal?

THIERRY: No big deal, just life.

(*A silence follows.*)

NANETTE: It's not like we are prying into your private life. What would it have cost you to email us and say you were coming here to

Peruwelz to meet us? Of course we appreciated the gesture, but it would have been nice to let us know.

THIERRY: Don't get hostile.

NANETTE: I am hostile! And hurt! We leave you alone and let you do whatever you please. But it's only a common courtesy to answer a few questions from your parents.

THIERRY: All in good time.

DANIEL: We're old, so we may not live that long. And, by the way, you're a married adult with a full-time job. Did you really expect us to send you pop tarts and beef jerky from America to France? Do you know how much it costs to send things overseas?

THIERRY: I'm worth it, aren't I?

NANETTE: No! Not to send junk food from the United States to France, for heaven's sake. Pop tarts and beef jerky, heck no!

THIERRY: Let's change the subject.

DANIEL: To what? Your job? That we don't even know if you still have? To your wife? Who won't communicate with us in French or English? To your living arrangements? You are still living in your mother-in-law's home, I suppose.

THIERRY: I may not pay rent, but we keep the place up and Elizabeth likes us to be there. Besides, I bought a new fridge, a new oven, a new microwave and a new garden gate. I picked up 500 kilos of apples and canned a hundred jars of vegetables and fruits . . .not just for me, but for my mother-in-law and whoever else wanted any.

DANIEL: That's very nice, but it's not rent and it's prolonging your dependency, which I consider unhealthy.

NANETTE: And all that work doesn't prevent you or Elizabeth from sending thank you notes for the things we have sent you both.

THIERRY: I keep telling Elizabeth that we need to send thank you notes, but your letters just sit there.

NANETTE: I'm certainly glad you're keeping up with your correspondence. At least you're talking about it and that's a step in the right direction. (*Pause.*) We have the feeling you don't want to be in touch, especially your wife. Does she not want to have any contact with us at all?

THIERRY: (*Hesitates.*) No, she really doesn't.

NANETTE and DANIEL: Why?

THIERRY: I don't really know. Maybe it has something to do with her childhood or being French, or not liking Americans. I don't know. She just doesn't want to know anything about either of you. It's better that way.

DANIEL: She married an American. What does that mean? (*Pauses.*) By the way, are you still working full time? Do you still have job?

THIERRY: Of course, and I like it. We go on the ships at Rouen and Dieppe, mostly grain shipments there. At Le Havre, it was mostly oil tankers, and they came in at every hour of the day and night. But at Rouen, the grain towers only operate during the daytime, so the hours are much more predictable. Also, because the grains, mostly wheat and soya beans, are susceptible to damage, they close the holds if there's any rain, which happens quite a bit.

NANETTE: So you don't have your apartment at Le Havre anymore?

THIERRY: No.

DANIEL: So why didn't you just say so when I asked you if you still liked your apartment? I don't understand. Your mother and I are direct people, honest people.

NANETTE: Yes, what you see is what you get.

DANIEL: So what's with the cat-and-mouse games, the half-truths, and the delayed revelations? It doesn't make sense. And it's not the way you we raised you. (*Pause.*) When exactly will we get the truth, the whole truth and nothing but the truth?

THIERRY: Everything in due time.

DANIEL: Due time? We're old. We'll die waiting.

NANETTE: Frankly, it's not our problem. Do what you want. You're a grown man. You're fully vaccinated. You're married and employed. (*Pauses.*) We're proud of your independence, it just seems that your withholding information is counter-productive.

THIERRY: Depending on the goal, of course.

DANIEL: Of course.

THIERRY: (*Pulls a car out of his wallet and hands it to DANIEL.*) Here it is.

NANETTE: What is it?

THIERRY: It's my Belgian *carte d'identité*. My proof of Belgian citizenship.

DANIEL: (*Examines the card.*) Ah, so now you don't have to stay married anymore. Is that it?

THIERRY: No! Of course not! I love Elizabeth and she loves me.

NANETTE: Well, you certainly have a curious relationship.

THIERRY: So do you two.

NANETTE: It's lasted 37 years, more than most marriages.

THIERRY: Congratulations!

DANIEL and NANETTE: Thank you.

THIERRY: I'm not interested in marital longevity, but happiness.

DANIEL and NANETTE: Happiness?

THIERRY: Yes, happiness. I don't want to find myself at 60, wondering how I wasted my life.

NANETTE: Happiness comes with independence, a good job, a decent home life and a meaningful contribution to society.

DANIEL: Happiness, if you achieve it, is a by-produce of a life well-lived, not a goal in itself.

THIERRY: I disagree and so does Elisabeth.

NANETTE: And your mother-in-law, what does she think?

THIERRY: Leave her out of this!

DANIEL: From the sounds of it, she's very active, both physically and mentally. She's involved in everything her town and region have to offer. We're not condemning her, but I would like to see you living on your own, in your own place.

THIERRY: Cool it! We've been over this before. (*Pause.*) By the way, I get to vote in the next Belgian elections.

NANETTE: You have to vote. It's obligatory in Belgium.

DANIEL: And for whom to you plan on voting?

THIERRY: That's my business.

DANIEL: (*Shrugs.*) More secrets, more mysteries. (*Raises his glass.*) I'd like to propose a toast. To our son, Thierry, man of mystery and to his lovely wife, Elizabeth, mistress of mysteries.

THIERRY: And to King Philippe, *Roi des Belges*, too?

DANIEL: Oh, you want to be more Belgian than the Belgians. Well Thierry, it won't work. You will improve your French and your European manners and you will stay a foreigner forever. That's the way it works. You can live here a hundred years and you will still be considered *l'américain.*

THIERRY: We'll see. (*Raises his glass.*) To Philippe, King of the Belgians, past, present and future. *Vive le Roi!*

ALL: (*Raise their glasses and chink them together.*) Santé!

(*Lights dim to dark.*)

THE END

FAMILY DYNAMICS

KNITTING PREMIE CAPS

MAKING CHRISTMAS WREATHS (THE DEAD)

GETTING A "B" IN FRENCH

GIVING A GIFT

LIBERATING GANDALF

THE BASS BOAT

ALLERGIC TO SEAFOOD

THE COLFAX MASSACRE

THE BEST PREDICTOR

THE MANUSCRIPT

KNITTING PREMIE CAPS

CAST OF CHARACTERS

PAULA: Young woman with a new-born baby

ELINOR: Paula's mother, a woman in her forties to fifties

NOTE: The ethnicity is not defined and may be any race.

SETTING

There are a couple of chairs and a crib, which is in the center of the stage.

(*PAULA puts the "baby" into the crib on its back. ELINOR is knitting a premie cap for a premature child.*)

ELINOR: Well, aren't you goin' to turn the baby over on its tummy?

PAULA: No, Mama. She's supposed to be on her back.

(*ELINOR stands and reaches in to turn the baby over. PAULA grabs ELINOR's hand and stops her.*)

PAULA: No! She's supposed to be on its back. Back to sleep! That's what the visiting nurse says.

ELINOR: (*Pulls back her hand.*) Why I never! Who told you such a silly thing?

PAULA: The visiting nurse, I said.

ELINOR: Well, she's wrong! I raised five children, includin' you, and they all slept on their stomachs. That's the natural way. It keeps 'em from spittin' up and swallowin' the vomit. Everyone knows that.

PAULA: That's changed. Now it's back to sleep and the nurse told me so.

ELINOR: You believe some silly stranger over your own mother?

PAULA: (*Hesitates.*) Yes, in this case, I do. It's based on re-search.

ELINOR: And suppose she's told you other lies and misinformation.

PAULA: Like what?

ELINOR: Like you should breast feed until your tits fall off and they you shouldn't sleep with your baby.

PAULA: Funny you should mention that. I am breast-feeding and I don't sleep with my baby.

ELINOR: See! I told you!

PAULA: So what?

ELINOR: You been gittin' a pack o'lies. You need to bond with your baby. Sleepin' with it gives you that skin-to-skin touch you both need. And breast-feedin' is okay, but not for months. (*Points to her own breasts.*) Look at these disasters! I'm ashamed to go out and when I do, I have to wear some super support bras just to keep these droopers off the floor. It's horrible.

PAULA: You breastfed for a year or more for all us kids, at least that's what you told me.

ELINOR: Yes, because I was too poor to buy formula and they didn't give it out like they do nowadays. Times was tough and we didn't have the choice. It was breastfeed or have your baby starve. It's not like that anymore. You got WIC. You can get formula just by askin'.

PAULA: (*Ignores ELINOR and puts the baby to her breast.*) I plan on nursing as long as I possibly can. And I don't care what it does to my breasts.

ELINOR: You may not care, but what about Darren. Do you think he's goin' to want to stick around and worship your body when you looks like some African villager?

PAULA: Darren loves me!

ELINOR: That's what your father said, too, until he ran out on all of us.

PAULA: Darren is not like that.

ELINOR: Really, so why hasn't he married you yet? It's his baby, isn't it?

PAULA: Of course it's his. (*Pauses.*) He hasn't married me because we both value our independence. He and I want some space in our togetherness, so we can grow.

ELINOR: Yes, and I bet he fills that space with a little somethin' on the side while you're raisin' a kid.

PAULA: Shut up! You're just jealous because Papa left you.

ELINOR: (*Continues to knit a cap.*) Maybe. Maybe not. (*Pauses.*) By the way, have you been tested for syphilis and HIV?

PAULA: You're disgusting!

ELINOR: Am I? I just read that the largest group of new HIV cases is in het-ero-sexual women.

PAULA: Read from where? The Daily Inquirer?

ELINOR: No, from an article in the newspaper, our local newspaper.

PAULA: Mama, don't make me believe you have started reading scientific articles anywhere. You're barely literate.

ELINOR: That's mean and untrue. I got through all of the "Fifty Shades of Gray" and the "Twilight" series, too.

PAULA: Right! The movie versions.

ELINOR: Well, I saw them. But they haven't even made a film of the "Fifty Shades of Gray" series yet, even though I plan on goin'.

PAULA: So who told you about the HIV numbers? And anyway, all pregnant women are tested for syphilis and HIV and I'm negative for both, in case you're interested.

ELINOR: Good! I'm glad to hear it. Just make sure Darren gets tested regular. You never know what the cat drags home after a night on the town.

PAULA: Speaking of cats, did you every get rid of that horrible yellow cat of yours, the one with blind eye and the missing right ear?

ELINOR: No, Baxter and I are doin' quite well together, thank you for askin'.

PAULA: Well, I can't do any more housesitting until you do get rid of him. The litter box might have toxoplasmosis. And I might be getting pregnant again soon.

ELINOR: Why?

PAULA: I like being pregnant. I like breastfeeding. And I like to get my welfare check.

ELINOR: Breastfeeding prevents pregnancy.

PAULA: Not always. Besides, I thought you wanted me to stop so my breasts would remain firm and beautiful.

ELINOR: Honey, birth control pills do the trick, and besides, I did breastfeedin' and it didn't stop me getting' pregnant with your brother.

PAULA: Which brother?

ELINOR: The one I aborted.

PAULA: I didn't know you did that.

ELINOR: There are a lot of things you don't know about me. (*Pauses in her knitting.*) So what about sharin' the bed with the baby. That's bad now, too? Eh?

PAULA: It's a leading cause of infant death, rollovers. Well second to abortion, of course, but that isn't any accident, is it?

ELINOR: No mother would roll over on her new baby.

PAULA: It happens all the time. Just like abortions, if that's what you really had.

ELINOR: Just like vomitin' and as-pir-ation pneumonia when you put babies on their backs. As-pir-ation, heard of that?

PAULA: Why did you get an abortion?

ELINOR: The child had con-gen-i-tal malformations. It almost didn't hardly have a brain and its heart was malformed. There was not way I was going to inflict that on you or myself. Besides, it was not goin' to be able to live.

PAULA: Love is not an infliction.

ELINOR: I could not offer that kind of time and energy to a handicapped child at the expense of time I needed to spend with you.

PAULA: He was one of God's children.

ELINOR: Yes, one of God's children. (*Pauses.*) But I can't solve the world's problems, face up or face down.

PAULA: (*Looks at what ELINOR is knitting.*) What are you knitting? It looks like a sock.

ELINOR: It's a premie cap.

PAULA: What for?

ELINOR: I do it for the children's hospital. It helps those teeny tiny babies who are born premature to keep in their body heat. (*Holds up the cap.*) Not much to look at, but they work good and it saves the hospital some money. I can make two or three a day if I'm not doin' anythin' else.

PAULA: That's a nice thing to do.

ELINOR: Thank you. I'm a nice person.

PAULA: (*Hugs ELINOR.*) I know, Mama, you mean well, but you just haven't kept up with the times.

ELINOR: Perhaps you're right. Maybe breast-feeding and back-to-sleep and are both good. Maybe co-sleepin' is bad. But I still slept with you, cradled you in my arms and dreamed of the family we were never goin' to have. I wanted you to have two parents and a stable address and no movin' and turbulence and evictions. (*Pauses.*) I wanted you kids to have a better life than I had. And I think you got it, at least most of it.

PAULA: Mama, you gave me a wonderful childhood. I didn't even think about those things then and now I have a baby of my own. Who cares if I'm on welfare?

ELINOR: Lots of people do. When you go to the supermarket and pull out those food stamps. You'll get all those mean, ugly stares. And when you try and get an apartment and you have to live in the HUD housing. That ain't no picnic neither.

PAULA: I won't care as long as my baby has food and we have a clean, safe place to live. I'll go back to school and get a good job and you can take care of my baby while I get my diploma and a really nice high-paying career.

ELINOR: Yes, that would be right nice. And maybe Darren can marry you and be a decent, God-fearin' man who supports his wife and child. Maybe that'll happen, too. (*Pauses.*) You should learn to make these things. (*Holds up the premie cap.*)

PAULA: Sure, why not? It's a nice thing to do. Give me those things. (*Takes the knitting needles and the yarn.*) How do you start?

ELINOR: You take the needles like this and catch onto the loops of yarn, like this.

(*Lights dim to dark.*)

THE END

MAKING CHRISTMAS WREATHS (THE DEAD)

CAST OF CHARACTERS

SHARON: Middle-aged woman. Well-dressed and correct speech patterns.

BETH: Middle-aged woman. Sloppier dress and speech patterns. Perhaps an old hippy appearance, with long, gray hair.

SETTING

There is a table and Sharon and Beth are working at making Christmas wreaths. They tie on red ribbons. The women may be seated or standing behind the table. There may be a couple of boxes with uncompleted wreaths and some boxes of completed ones.

(*SHARON and BETH are working on Christmas wreaths.*)

SHARON: (*Holds up a wreath.*) How does this one look?

BETH: Fine.

SHARON: Don't you think the bow's a bit too large?

BETH: No, it looks fine.

SHARON: Is it crooked? I think it's a little too much to the right.

BETH: (*Slightly angry.*) No, Sharon! It's not too big, not too small and not crooked. It's perfect. (*Pauses.*) For heaven's sake, what's it matter? It's for dead people anyway.

SHARON: (*Slams down her wreath.*) Beth Sheppard! These are for deceased veterans and we owe them the respect they earned through their service to our country. Don't be disrespectful!

BETH: Sorry.

(*BETH and SHARON work in silence for a few seconds.*)

SHARON: Did you hear about Dorothy's mother's ashes?

BETH: No, what?

SHARON: Well, Dorothy had her mother cremated and then her ashes got stuck somewhere in the cheap seats at the columbarium.

BETH: Really?

SHARON: Yes, really. And then one of Dorothy's great aunts wanted to know just what happened to the ashes, so she called Dorothy and they finally tracked them down. They were stuck up on a shelf in the back of building with a sign marked "Pending final disposition."

BETH: (*Laughs.*) That's pretty funny.

SHARON: (*Serious.*) What's funny about it?

BETH: There's nothin' more final than death, followed by cremation. Except of course if you're one of those people who have their ashes made into a ceramic raku jug by a pot maker.

SHARON: That can't be true.

BETH: Yes it is! And when I go, you can turn me into a big vase and stuff flowers into me from time to time. I think it would be cool.

SHARON: You're disgusting.

BETH: No. It's a nice idea. (*Works on her wreath.*) What'll I care, anyway? I'll be dead.

SHARON: You may not care, but I will. I'll make sure there is registry somewhere and that your descendants will know exactly which pot you're in and where it ends up. I swear I will!

BETH: No need to swear. I believe you. (*Holds up her completed wreath.*) How does this one look?

SHARON: If that's the best you can do, I guess it's okay.

BETH: (*Takes another wreath to tie on a bow.*) Did you hear about Raymond's brother, Charlie?

SHARON: No, what about him.

BETH: He lost his apartment, his car, his wife, and his child. All within a year.

SHARON: What happened this time.

BETH: Drugs again.

SHARON: Which one this time. I hear heroin's big this year.

BETH: I don't know. Someone said it was Krocodil or something nasty like that. (*Works on her wreath.*) He's been in and out of rehab for the last few years.

SHARON: I try not to follow too closely. He's a loser. He was loser in high school and he's a loser now.

BETH: He was a veteran, too.

SHARON: Yes, who got dishonorably discharged for drug use.

BETH: So he doesn't get a wreath, or even a site in the military cemetery when he dies?

SHARON: Of course not, you know that. Shooting yourself to death with God knows what drug and frying your brain is not the same thing as dying in the service of your country.

BETH: He said he had PTSD and that made him start drugs. He's also lost his left arm from shootin' up some nasty stuff. It went into an artery and his arm just sort of sloughed off. At least that's what his wife told me. She said the whole arm turned black and horrible and they just had to chop it off above the elbow. That's before she left him. Not because of the arm, but because she just couldn't take it anymore.

SHARON: Horrible. It's all horrible. (*Works on her wreath.*) So what is his wife doing?

BETH: She's strugglin'. She gets a little somethin' from his disability check. And she has a part-time job at the Wal-Mart. She and her son live over in the Shadelands Subdivision.

SHARON: That's not a nice place at all.

BETH: No, it's pretty dangerous and the school district is terrible.

SHARON: She shouldn't have married Charlie.

BETH: Maybe, but she was pregnant and he was goin' into the army. It seemed like a good idea at the time, I suppose. (*Works on her wreath. Completes the bow and shows it to SHARON.*) Can we put aside a wreath for Charlie's wife? I'm sure she won't be buyin' any decorations for Christmas. And maybe even one for Charlie's half-way house,

SHARON: Of course not! These are for the veteran's only.

BETH: Come on, Sharon. One or two wreaths won't make any difference. Charlie's just about dead anyway.

SHARON: Certainly not!

BETH: That halfway house of his will probably need a little Christmas cheer.

SHARON: Stop! (*Puts down her wreath.*) Good God-fearing, patriotic people donated money to honor our war dead with Christmas wreaths. Doing anything else with them would be sacrilegious.

BETH: But the livin' need them more than the dead.

SHARON: The dead ones are the deserving here, not the ungrateful living.

BETH: (*Reaches out and touches SHARON.*) Sharon, Charlie's you're nephew. He needs some compassion, too. He might get a tiny shred of pleasure from a wreath on the door. Can we re-focus our energy here a little bit?

SHARON: NO!

BETH: (*Takes a twenty dollar bill from her pocket.*) Here's a twenty. I'll buy two wreaths from you. You can replace them.

SHARON: No! It's dishonest.

BETH: (*Sets the money on the table. Continues to work on a wreath.*) You know what Jesus said?

SHARON: Don't take the Lord's name in vain!

BETH: I'm not!

SHARON: Is this some sort of perverse knock-knock joke?

BETH: No, I swear.

SHARON: (*Reconsiders.*) Okay, what did Jesus say?

BETH: (*Sets down her wreath.*) He told his disciples "follow me and let the dead bury the dead."

SHARON: Jesus said that?

BETH: Yes, he did.

SHARON: What does that mean anyway?

BETH: I'm no religious expert, but I think it means that the people who are spiritually dead are the ones that should take care of those that are already physically dead. I think it's a metaphor.

SHARON: Beth, I didn't realize you were so philosophical.

BETH: Yeah, you just thought I was dumb and superficial. I knew I've heard you say that to your husband.

SHARON: (*Works on the wreath.*) I'm sorry. I didn't mean it even if I said it.

BETH: That's okay. I can be pretty dense sometime.

SHARON: (*Works in silence a few minutes.*) Have I become so hard-hearted? So misdirected?

BETH: (*Pauses.*) Yes, pretty much.

SHARON: (*Looks around.*) I guess I can buy a couple of replacement wreaths. (*Takes the money and hands it and a couple of wreaths to BETH.*) Take the money back and take these two wreaths. Give one to Charlie's ex-wife and take the other one over to his halfway house. If anyone asks you, just say they come from some veteran's organization.

BETH: No, I'll tell them they are from you.

SHARON: No, please don't. I've turned Charlie away time after time. It was just too hard. He's an emotional and economic black hole who sucks everything down. He'll probably sell the wreath and get some dope.

BETH: Maybe. (*Takes the wreaths.*) And maybe he'll realize it was a gift from a merciful generous person, maybe even a relative, who still cares about him even though he has squandered his life.

SHARON: Don't tell either of them it comes from me. It would break my heart if they knew. I've told Charlie's wife to her face that she was a stupid little whore, in front of her child. It's all too much to think about. (*Returns to making a wreath.*) At least the dead leave me in peace. Maybe that's why I'm so comfortable with them.

BETH: Yes, but the livin' really need you, not the dead.

SHARON: Please go quickly. I might change my mind. And don't tell them. It would break my heart.

BETH: (*Leaving.*) I'll hurry up and be back in a couple of hours to help you put the wreaths at the veteran's cemetery.

SHARON: (*Smiles.*) Drive carefully and don't hurry. (*BETH leaves.*) I think the dead can wait a little longer for their wreaths. They won't care and I shouldn't either. (*Shakes her head. Mutters to herself.*) Let the dead bury the dead. I'll be damned.

THE END

GETTING A "B" IN FRENCH

CAST OF CHARACTERS

RAYMOND: Late 50's. May be balding or slightly overweight. Casually dressed. Correct, un-accented speech pattern.

EMILY: Raymond's daughter, early 20's. Casually dressed, but more student-like.

SETTING

Living room or dining room setting. Casual, no fancy furniture or complicated set elements.

RAYMOND: You can't get a "B," not in French! That's you're minor, for heaven's sake.

EMILY: I did. I got a "B" and I was glad to get that, Dad. Have you ever tied to write an essay about existentialism in French using the *passé-simple*?

RAYMOND: I don't know what "*passé- simple*" is.

EMILY: It's the literary past tense in French that is used only in writing and never in spoken French, like some sort of dead verb tense.

RAYMOND: It doesn't matter. It's something you should know if you're taking advanced level courses.

EMILY: They stuck me in that advanced class. It's where they thought I should be because of my high school classes and my language testing. And it's as hard as hell! (*Pauses.*) It's filled with nerds that are practically linguists; at least the ones that are passing. The others have just dropped out because the teacher's a bitch and just too hard.

RAYMOND: Don't use that sort of language, young lady! And maybe you should drop out, too. It's not worth ruining your grade point average for a course like that.

EMILY: Ruining my grade average? Are you crazy?

RAYMOND: Don't talk to your father like that!

EMILY: Sorry, but I still have a 3.5 grade average, even with a "B" in French. And that's in one of the most prestigious universities in the South; at least that's what you keep telling me.

RAYMOND: It is prestigious and expensive and I graduated from there.

EMILY: So that makes it good.

RAYMOND: (*Ignores the remark.*) Emily, honey, when you go for a graduate program or an internship that only accepts 25 students from all over the world, they will take the ones with a 3.9 grade average and not the ones with the 3.5. They won't even look at someone with a 3.5. You'll see that I'm right.

EMILY: Then maybe that's not what I want to do? Maybe that's not what I should do?

RAYMOND: Maybe if you spent more time in the library and less out drinking with your college buddies, you'd be getting that "A" in French.

EMILY: (*Angrily.*) I worked as hard as I could. And I don't want to waste my youth in the library like some sort of nun in a convent.

RAYMOND: Or a monk in a monastery, like me? Is that what you mean?

EMILY: No, I didn't mean to be insulting. I know you studied a lot. But you had to have had some fun, too, didn't you?

RAYMOND: No, I didn't. I studied day and night and I got those "A's" when I needed them to get into medical school And I got into medical school when those guys with their 3.5's didn't. (*Points to himself.*) I got in and those other losers didn't.

EMILY: So, I'm a loser now?

RAYMOND: (*Hugs her.*) Of course not! You're my darling, intelligent little girl. I just don't want you to be doing some sort of dead-end job in some God-forsaken little town in the middle of nowhere and be stuck there for forty years wondering what happened.

EMILY: Because I didn't get an "A" in advanced French literature?

RAYMOND: Precisely.

EMILY: Maybe I wouldn't mind living in a little town in the middle of nowhere, earning a living and doing some good for the local society.

RAYMOND: Society of peasants, like Tolstoy, I suppose. You'll be slumming with the rednecks while your beautiful, clever brain rots away in your head. (*Shakes his head.*) No, not while I'm around!

EMILY: And what are you going to do exactly? Are you going to take my French class for me? How are you going to fill me with that same incredible dedication and drive that you have?

RAYMOND: I hoped that you would have gotten that from me, or have at least learned by example.

EMILY: What example? Working day and night, working weekends and on vacations? Missing my ballet recitals, my school plays, my soccer matches, all because you were busy doing something so important with all those other people, those very important patients. Is that the example you wanted to give me?

RAYMOND: Yes! It was important! And it's still important! And now I can bask in the adulations of my patients, my peers and the community, and be paid for doing it. Is that so bad?

EMILY: And your family?

RAYMOND: (*Pauses.*) I don't need your adulation, or even your respect. But I do need your love.

EMILY: Even from a loser daughter with a "B" in French.

RAYMOND: (*Hugs EMILY.*) Drop the course. Save your GPA.

EMILY: (*Pushes RAYMOND away.*) You don't get it, do you?

RAYMOND: Get what?

EMILY: That I don't care if I get an "A" or a "B." A "B's" okay and maybe a "B" is all I can do. And maybe I'm just a "B" kind of girl.

RAYMOND: Not in my family! We may have our faults, but mediocrity is not one of them.

EMILY: Dad, let's put things in perspective, please. (*Pauses.*) Why don't you sit down?

RAYMOND: (*Sits. Jokingly.*) Is it that bad?

EMILY: I went to the school doctor a week or so ago because I was seeing double.

RAYMOND: Yes. And?

EMILY: I thought it was just fatigue from too much studying.

RAYMOND: Or too many late nights with the friends?

EMILY: (*Ignores RAYMOND.*) So the doctor orders some tests and has me get a CAT scan of the brain.

RAYMOND: (*More concerned.*) Why didn't you tell your mom and me?

EMILY: No need to bother you until I had something to share.

RAYMOND: (*Pulls EMILY down beside him.*) And?

EMILY: The CT scan shows I've got a brain tumor.

RAYMOND: You're joking? (*Pauses.*) You're just angry with me. This is some sort of sadistic joke, isn't it?

EMILY: No, it's not. I wish it were. (*Pauses.*) They need to do a brain biopsy to find out what kind of tumor it is. But the neurologists thinks it's probably a glioblastoma because of my age and the way it looks on the scan.

RAYMOND: We'll get a second opinion. This can't be right. We need to go to a specialized center, to the Mayo Clinic or the Cleveland Clinic or Johns-Hopkins.

EMILY: Why? I'm going to one of the best schools in the South. You picked it out. You went there, too. The medical school is world famous. Why would I go somewhere else?

RAYMOND: (*Hugs EMILY.*) Oh, honey. I'm so sorry. I'm worried. I'm scared. I'm so sorry I gave you trouble about a grade in French. I don't know what came over me. You're right, so right. We'll get through this together. First, we'll get the biopsy and talk to the specialists and get a plan of action. French, what was I thinking? What a fool I've been. (*Hugs EMILY again.*) Can you forgive me, honey? Please tell me you can forgive me and we can work through this together.

EMILY: (*Takes RAYMOND's hand and kisses it.*) It's okay, Dad.

RAYMOND: No, it's not okay. It's a nightmare. Have you talked to your mother about this yet?

EMILY: Not yet.

RAYMOND: Don't do it yet! Not now, anyway. Let's make sure what this thing is. It might not even be malignant. Maybe there's a cure or it's resectable? There are some terrific neuro-surgeons here, world famous specialists.

EMILY: Dad, don't be mad?

RAYMOND: Mad at what? (*Hugs EMILY.*) My angel, my precious darling, what could you do that would make me mad?

EMILY: (*Stands up and moves away a few feet.*) I don't have a brain tumor.

RAYMOND: (*Confused.*) What do you have?

EMILY: I don't have anything wrong with me physically?

RAYMOND: And mentally? I don't care what it is; we can work through this together?

EMILY: I don't have anything wrong with me at all. I was just making it up.

RAYMOND: (*Stunned.*) What! (*Angrily. Stands to confront EMILY.*) Why would you do something like that to me? That's cruel! That's abusive! I didn't raise you to act that way. Lying to your father, and about something like that? It's despicable!

EMILY: Aren't you glad I don't have a brain tumor?

RAYMOND: (*Sits down. Pulls EMILY over next to him. Strokes EMILY's hair.*) Oh yes! Yes, I'm so glad! I'm so relieved. Oh, thank God!

EMILY: But I did get a "C" in French, not a "B."

RAYMOND: A "C?"

EMILY: Yes.

RAYMOND: I don't know what to say.

EMILY: (*Hugs him.*) That's good for a change! Don't say anything. And a "C" is not the end of the world. I'm not dying. In twenty years, no one will care or remember what I got in Advanced French. (*Stands up and gestures.*) And in the great cosmic scheme of things, it won't really matter, will it?

RAYMOND: (*Stands and hugs EMILY.*) No, Honey, it won't matter. (*Backs up and looks at EMILY.*) You're smart. You're smarter than I ever was and ever will be.

EMILY: "Honor thy father and mother that your days will be long on earth."

RAYMOND: That's a good commandment, Em. But please remember the "Thou shalt not lie" one as well. Don't do anything like that, every again. Promise?

EMILY: I promise. (*Reaches into her pocket and pulls out a package of Gummy Bears.*) You want a Gummy Bear?

RAYMOND: (*Takes the package and sits down. Pulls out a Gummy Bear.*) My favorites are still the red ones.

EMILY: (*Sits down beside him and takes a Gummy Bear.*) I like the yellow ones, myself. (*Hands the package back to RAYMOND.*) Another?

RAYMOND: Thanks. (*Takes a Gummy Bear.*)

   (*Lights dim to dark.*)

THE END

GIVING A GIFT

103

CAST OF CHARACTERS

ANITA: Female physician, casually but correctly dressed. Speaks English without an accent. She is Brad's wife.

BRAD: Male physician. Casually dressed. He may even be in scrubs. May speak with a slight foreign accent. He is Anita's husband.

SETTING

Minimal set elements. Perhaps a couple of chairs or a sofa, with a coffee table and oriental carpet. There can be some contemporary art on the walls. There is a wrapped gift on the table.

(ANITA is finishing wrapping a gift. She shows it to BRAD, who is sitting in one of the chairs and reading a newspaper or magazine.)

ANITA: (*Shows the gift to BRAD.*) Well, do you like it?

BRAD: The wrapping is very nice. Am I supposed to know what's inside?

ANITA: No, but it's Dorothy's gift, of course.

BRAD: (*Without conviction.*) Nice. (*Goes back to reading.*)

ANITA: (*Offended.*) Nice? Is that it? It's a Coach purse that cost me a pretty penny.

BRAD: She's a bit young for such an extravagant gift, isn't she?

ANITA: Thirteen? That's not so young. Have you even looked at your daughter lately? She's getting to be an attractive young lady. And she's very sensitive to fashion.

BRAD: (*Shrugs her shoulders.*) Yes, she's getting some breast development. But that doesn't make her a young lady. (*Pauses.*) By the way, I'm sure she'd be happier if you could actually be there at her birthday party, with or without a gift. I think she probably gets that from me.

ANITA: (*Angrily.*) You know I can't be there! I'm on call this weekend.

BRAD: And you couldn't switch with someone?

ANITA: Switch! With one of those bastards at the clinic? They'd find every excuse to not help me out, and even if they did switch, they'd make me pay with a pound of flesh.

BRAD: And blood. Don't forget the blood. Shylock already made that mistake.

ANITA: Yes, let's not forget the blood. And I'm sure they wouldn't either. (*Pauses.*) By the way, I'm not Shylock.

BRAD: (*Pauses.*) Why don't you just quit practice? You could so something part time.

ANITA: Quit? After struggling to get into medical school, then struggling to get through residency and then struggling to hold my own with a bunch of misogynous assholes.

BRAD: Anatomical, always so anatomical. Perhaps you can choose a non-body part for your next description. It's just too medical.

ANITA: Pricks! How about that?

BRAD: Still too anatomical.

ANITA: Sons of bitches.

BRAD: Better, but insulting to their mothers?

ANITA: (*Sighs.*) I just can't quit practicing. It's too important to me and I really do like helping people. And they appreciate me. I just couldn't turn my back on all that. I have to remain relevant.

BRAD: You want me to quit?

ANITA: Of course not. You're a pillar of every medical committee in the hospital, plus the Chief of Staff, plus President of the Medical Society and God knows what else.

BRAD: So?

ANITA: So, why would you throw away years of training and expertise? You'd go crazy being a stay-at-home dad and I would be working harder than ever at the hospital. What good would that do?

BRAD: Maybe I would know exactly what to do at home? (*Pauses.*) Have you ever thought that this rat race might just be killing me, too?

ANITA: A bit dramatic, no?

BRAD: An ER doctor called me at two a.m. the other night from one of those out-lying rural hospitals. You know the one.

ANITA: I can guess.

BRAD: I listened to the story and then all I could ask was why in the hell it took them ten hours to figure out that someone needed to be transferred to a larger hospital. Then I yelled, "Just transfer the patient if you can manage to do that!" and I slammed down the receiver.

ANITA: So?

BRAD: That was my honored colleague on the other end of the line.

ANITA: Really? If he was so honored, why couldn't he figure out how to transfer a patient in a timely way?

BRAD: She.

ANITA: Ah. (*Pauses and picks up the gift.*) How many birthday parties, parent-teacher meetings, dance recitals, and God knows what else I've missed with Dorothy over the years. (*Shakes her head.*) I'm a rotten mother.

BRAD: No you're not. You're a mediocre mother and a very good doctor.

ANITA: Thanks. (*Looks at the gift.*) What will Dorothy say when she's 18 or 20 or 35? Will she even still be speaking with me at that point?

BRAD: Of course she will be. I'm still talking to you and we've been living together longer than that.

ANITA: Brad, be serious for once. (*Steps over and gives him a hug.*) I'll just keep going on and sacrificing myself on the altar of medicine, but for what?

BRAD: Because your patients love you.

ANITA: Yes, but they pass away and get buried while my daughter remains. . .at least for the time being. (*Pauses.*) Does it have to be so hard? Do I always have to choose between my daughter's birthday party and a night on call? Do I have to choose between being a decent parent and a decent doctor?

BRAD: Right now, it looks like that's choice.

ANITA: How can those old docs around here just keep going and going? Up all night, working all day, working all weekend. How do they do it? They can stay up 24 hours a day over and over and still look like they just stepped off the golf course. How in hell do they do it?

BRAD: Viagra?

ANITA: Oh, for heaven's sake. That's not it.

BRAD: Cialis?

ANITA: (*Ignores the comment. Shakes her head and frowns.*) Right. And maybe they use meth while they're at it.

BRAD: Do you admire them, those old doctors? Do you want to follow in their footsteps?

ANITA: Part of me does. Part of me admires their stamina and dedication. But another part asks what did they sacrifice during their lifetimes? What about their wives and children? What did they give up?

BRAD: Most of their kids went on to medical school.

ANITA: Yes, they did. And it just keeps going on and on, the same bad version of Ground Hog Day.

BRAD: Maybe Frank will take call for you. He seems pretty nice. He asks about Dorothy from time to time and that's more than I can say about any of the others.

ANITA: (*Picks up the gift.*) A Coach purse and a David Yurman bracelet. How much money do I have to spend to overcome my sense of guilt?

BRAD: None! (*Takes the gift.*) Save this for Christmas and go to Dorothy's party. I'll take call for you.

ANITA: You can't.

BRAD: Why not?

ANITA: Because you're exhausted, too. You can barely keep your eyes open and you're not even in the same medical specialty. (*Shakes her head.*) I appreciate the noble gesture, but you just can't take call for me. That's ridiculous.

BRAD: I want to see you happy. I want to see you fulfilled. I want you to feel you're a good mother, but you always have to be the best at everything. (*Pauses.*) It's just not possible. You can't be the best mother in the world and the best doctor in town. (*Pauses. Strokes ANITA's hair.*) Just be okay. I'll still love you. (*Takes ANITA in his arms.*) Be an okay doctor and an okay mother, that's fine, too.

ANITA: (*Pulls away.*) And when I get dragged into court because I was just an okay doctor, are you going to protect me there, too? We have to be the best doctor's in the world. Nobody is held to those standards and if we have a bad outcome, we end up in court in front of some sleazy plaintiff's attorney who will tell us just how rotten we are.

BRAD: Everything doesn't end up in court. (*Pauses.*) It doesn't have to. Not even divorce.

ANITA: Divorce? What are you saying? Are your considering divorce after all of the tenderness you've been exuding. You just said you wanted me to be happy and fulfilled and now you're talking about divorce. You're joking aren't you?

BRAD: (*Sighs. Quietly.*) No, I'm not joking.

ANITA: (*Looks at BRAD.*) You're really serious, aren't you?

BRAD: Yes. (*Steps to the side.*) I've done the best I could. I wanted to love you. I've always admired you. I did love you. But fighting for scraps of time just isn't enough for me anymore either. You've missed more than dance recitals and parent-teacher conferences over the years. There hasn't been five minutes of real sustained tenderness in the past five years. It's too much.

ANITA: Divorce? For real?

BRAD: Yes.

ANITA: Is there someone else?

BRAD: Yes.

ANITA: Who?

BRAD: That's not important.

ANITA: (*Screams and slams the gift to the floor.*) Not important! You're just like the rest of them. You've sucked me dry for thirty years and now you'll leave me like an ugly, wrinkled shell. (*Pauses.*) This is a joke, isn't it?

BRAD: No, Anita, it's not. (*Walks away.*) And if you can make it to Dorothy's party one way or another, I'm sure she'll appreciate it. (*Picks up the gift from the floor.*) And don't forget this. (*Hands ANITA the gift.*) Maybe it's the best you can do right now.

ANITA: (*Pulls back her hand to slap BRAD.*) You hypocritical monster! You're worse than all of them. At least they just fucked me emotionally and financially. You were doing it physically as well!

BRAD: Not that much lately, in case you haven't noticed.

ANITA: You're a monster! Get out of here and never come back! Go to your whore, whoever she is, and screw her until her eyes fall out if that's what you like.

BRAD: I'm too tired for that, too. (*Pauses.*) Go to Dorothy's party. Call your colleagues and tell them you're sick. Tell them you're too sick to work and too sick to be a decent mother as well. Maybe they can relate to that. (*Walks off the stage.*)

ANITA: (*Takes the gift and hugs it, and then she slumps down, shaking her head. Her cell phone goes off and she looks at it.*) Yes. (*Pauses.*) Yes. I'm on my way. Go ahead and give him some fresh frozen plasma and six units of platelets. I'll be right there. (*Exits, leaving the gift on the couch.*)

THE END

LIBERATING GANDALF

CAST OF CHARACTERS

JACK: Early middle-aged man, dressed in casual clothes, perhaps a bit rumpled. May be slightly overweight, with some pre-mature balding.

HENRIETTA: Jack's mother. An older woman, dressed in an ugly housecoat and slippers. Her hair is pulled back in a bun, or even in curlers.

SETTING

In the center of a bare stage is a large, tall box, almost as big as a person. It is the size of a refrigerator box. It is made of wood or sturdy carton and is mounted on a base with casters so it can be moved and pivoted around without falling down.

JACK: (*Pushes the box into stage center in front of HENRIETTA. Makes a flourishing gesture.*) Ta da!

HENRIETTA: (*Looks at the box.*) What is it?

JACK: More appropriately, who is it?

HENRIETTA: Okay, don't play games with me, young man. Who is it?

JACK: I'm your son, not some random young man. (*Points to the box.*) And this is a three quarter scale replica of Gandalf, the Wizard.

HENRIETTA: Who?

JACK: Gandalf, the Wizard, from J.R.R. Tolkien's "The Lord of the Rings."

HENRIETTA: That book?

JACK: Yes, those books. Four of them counting "The Hobbit." And five if you add "The Silmarillion."

HENRIETTA: That's very nice; now get that thing out of here right now!

JACK: What?

HENRIETTA: You heard me. I said get that thing out of this house. We have enough useless, ugly junk around here, including your deadbeat dad. And I don't want some hideous life-size statue of a magician or whoever this it supposed to be.

JACK: (*Goes over and touches the box tenderly.*) This is a polished pewter statue with semi-precious stones incrusted in the eyes and on his staff.

HENRIETTA: You mean this thing is naked? Like a statue of David with jewels on its phallus? That's disgusting!

JACK: Of course not! His staff is a kind of magical stick he's holding, not his penis. For heaven's sake, Mother, you can be so vulgar and perverted.

HENRIETTA: No, I'm not perverted, you are. This monstrosity, whatever it looks like, needs to be out of this house by tomorrow. It won't fit anywhere, even in a closet. And I'm sure it won't match the interior decorating, either.

JACK: (*Laughs.*) Right! That's probably true. It's not really early trailer trash and it won't match your Kincaid Master of Light print of a New England cottage. (*Points to an imaginary or real painting.*) Now that's really trash and ought to be out of here. While this, (*touches the box*) is a real work of art!

HENRIETTA: How much did you pay for this piece of junk? (*Pushes the box, which spins slightly.*) It's heavy.

JACK: That's right, nearly fifty pounds of pure metallic beauty.

HENRIETTA: And the cost?

JACK: That's none of your business!

HENRIETTA: It is my house and you are my son and it certainly is my business.

JACK: Okay, you want to know how much it costs. (*Comes over and whispers something in HENRIETA's ear.*) There, satisfied?

HENRIETTA: What! You spend that kind of money on some sort of toy while you know we need a new roof, a new dishwasher, and a new car. (*Starts to wail dramatically.*) Oh Jack, how could you?

JACK: It's my money and you just said it's your house. Why should I even want to repair your roof?

HENRIETTA: Because you live here, too, rent-free. No responsibilities, your clothes are washed and dried, you have two meals a day and you come and go when you please. You lead the life of Riley while I slave here taking care of you and your father. And you spend a fortune on some fantasy action figure?

JACK: (*Goes over and caresses the box.*) Nothing's free in life. You get what you pay for. (*Pauses.*) Sure, I come and go as I please, but I'm suffocating under the weight of my filial obligations. I can't breathe. I'm dying in this hellhole.

HENRIETA: Watch your tongue, boy. You know what the Good Book says, "Honor your father and mother that your days may be long on earth."

JACK: (*Comes over and touches HENRIETTA's shoulder.*) I do honor you. And I do benefit from your generosity. But if I can't leave, at least I want something of mine here. (*Points to the box.*) This is a part of me. It's a part of my psychic self, a soul brother of sorts.

HENRIETTA: (*Stops weeping abruptly.*) Oh, come on! It sounds like this statue is your lover. (*Pauses.*) In fact, I'd much rather you bring a girlfriend or even a boyfriend home than this useless cold, piece of junk.

JACK: Mother, you can be so twisted.

HENRIETTA: Am I? Prove me wrong.

JACK: You say that sort of thing and yet you would treat a flesh and blood lover with the same contempt as you're heaping on this statue. Why do you think I don't dare bring anyone here to meet you? (*Touches the box.*) Except Gandalf.

HENRIETTA: Stop it! I have always been nurturing to you and welcoming to your friends. Don't you dare use me as an excuse for your social shortcomings! You're an intellectual giant and an emotional dwarf and I always told your dad. . . .

JACK: (*Cuts her off.*) Shut up! (*Raises his hand to hit HENRIETTA.*)

HENRIETTA: Hitting your mother? Is that what you want to do? (*Shows her cheek and point to it.*) Here, go ahead. Give me a big wallop. Knock me down. Kill me!

JACK: (*Lowers his hand.*) I'm sorry. (*Goes to the box.*) Maybe it is time I left home. I can take Gandalf and we'll find a little condominium not far from my work.

HENRIETTA: (*Laughs.*) And use your ridiculous statue as a garden gnome, perhaps?

JACK: No, as a centerpiece in my living room. (*Pauses.*) They have a place over on Masonic for less than $1,000 a month. They want a security deposit of $500. I already have a copy of a lease. I can certainly afford a place of my own; I make good money.

HENRIETTA: Yes, you do. And you've been able to save your money as well, thanks to me and your father.

JACK: You don't really want Gandalf or me here anymore. You think I'm a social degenerate. (*Pauses.*) Then it's time we should be leaving. (*Pushes the statue toward stage right.*) Let's go, Gandalf. We know when we're not wanted.

HENRIETTA: No! Stop! (*Catches the edge of the box and spins it around.*)

JACK: Why?

HENRIETTA: Because we need you.

JACK: What for? I don't do anything. I don't pay rent. I don't buy food or cook. I don't even work in the yard. Why do you want me to stay?

HENRIETTA: (*Releases the box and gives JACK a hug.*) Because you're my little boy, my Little Jack Horner. (*Caresses his head.*) You give me a reason to get up in the morning and make breakfast, to clean the house, to do the laundry, to fix dinner. (*Looks at her watch.*) I look at the clock at noon and know you're eating with your colleagues at work. And by three, I know you're having coffee. By 4:30, I began to feel tinges of anticipation knowing you're driving home. My rituals depend on you; they turn around you. You are the sun and I am a planet.

JACK: And Dad?

HENRIETTA: Your father has always been a distant, cold, reclusive person. Now he hardly ever leaves his room. He's the past, but you're the present and the future.

JACK: And what about that "come grow old with me, the best is yet to be" stuff. That doesn't hold true for you and dad?

HENRIETTA: That best is long gone. There's only the prospect of endless days of silence and boredom. It's all gone, except for you. (*Touches the box and grabs it with both hands.*) And Gandalf.

   (*Jack grabs the other side of the box and it begins to pivot slowly, as if JACK and HENRIETTA are dancing a slow, perverse waltz.*)

JACK: That sounds more like something a lover would say to a lover, not a mother to her son.

HENRIETTA: (*Continues to move the box rhythmically.*) Oh, Little Jack. Even as a boy, you were petulant and self-willed. It took forever to train you to be obedient.

JACK: Like a puppy?

HENRIETTA: No, of course not! (*Waltzes with the box, pushing it in JACK's direction.*) Keep it! You can keep Gandalf, but you have to put it in your own room.

JACK: (*Surprised. Stops the motion.*) Really? You'll really let me keep him.

HENRIETTA: Yes, really. (*Caresses the box.*) A friend of yours is a friend of mine. (*Embraces the box and give it a quick kiss.*) I'll love Gandalf like I love you, with the same maternal passion and the same familial lust.

JACK: (*Pushes the box and backs away.*) Get off, you pervert! Leave Gandalf and me alone! I'll sign that lease. I'll finally get out of here.

HENRIETTA: (*Backs away momentarily and then goes back to the box and caresses it.*) No! No, please no! I'm not perverted. I'm just starting to share one of your obsessive interests. I'm bonding with Gandalf.

JACK: It's a statue! (*Pushes her away again.*) Get off1

HENRIETTA: We're one, you and I, united with an unbreakable spiritual bond.

JACK: (*Pauses and considers.*) Can I put Gandalf in the den?

HENRIETTA: By the window, not in the middle.

JACK: And no covers on him or anything.

HENRIETTA: (*Pauses. Sighs.*) Okay, Gandalf can stay if you do.

JACK: Okay. I'll stay, even though I should really leave the place. (*Looks around.*)

HENRIETTA: (*Stokes JACK'S cheek.*) Ah, my Little Jack Horner stuck in the corner, eating his curds and whey.

JACK: Doesn't Gandalf get any affection?

HENRIETTA: Okay, for you, too, Mr. Wizard. (*Kisses the box with a lingering kiss.*) Now let's go to the kitchen. I've got a nice chicken salad on a bed of organic spinach and your favorite banana pudding for dessert.

(*HENRIETTA and JACK begin to exit.*)

JACK: And Gandalf?

HENRIETTA: I think he'll be all right for a while. We'll take him out of the box after lunch. (*With a touch of irony.*) I really want to see that jewel incrusted staff. (*Gives a wink, and then takes JACK by the shoulder and leads him off stage.*)

(*Lights dim to dark with the box in the center of the stage.*)

THE END

THE BASS BOAT

CAST OF CHARACTERS

GEORGE: Young adult, country demeanor and Southern rural accent

BETTY: George's wife. Milder country accent. Casually dressed.

SETTING

Minimal set, with a table, a couple of chairs. Nothing elaborate. Some knitting materials and some books on the table.

GEORGE: (*Holds up a pink slip. Waves it in the air.*) Shit! (*Hands it to BETTY.*) I'd hoped they'd wait until next year before they fired us all.

BETTY: (*Looks at the paper. Hands it back to GEORGE.*) I'm sorry. I know you thought it might happen, but it's still got to be devastating. (*Tries to give him a hug.*)

GEROGE: (*Pushes BETTY away.*) Don't be givin' me any of that psychological-social work book-learning crap! Feelings! Feelings! I feel screwed! That's what I feel. Twenty-five years at that hellhole of a factory and they close the place in less than a week. It's bullshit! Nasty bullshit!

BETTY: What difference would it have made to wait until next year?

GEORGE: Well, for one thing my damn bass boat would've been paid off. Then we would've just had the house and car notes. No, it's just too much at once.

BETTY: Sell the bass boat!

GEORGE: Come on! A four-year-old boat isn't worth a third of what I paid for it, even if it was in perfect shape. (*Pauses.*) Mine's already has serious engine problems and a dinged up paint job. And don't forget the cracked windshield. Everyone's like me; they want what I wanted, that new boat smell, like a car has. They want the chrome to sparkle and no scratches or chips or dents anywhere. That's what I wanted back when I bought it and that's what everyone else still wants now.

BETTY: Was it worth it?

GEORGE: What?

BETTY: Buying the boat?

GEORGE: (*Pauses. Sighs.*) The day I bought that boat was one of the happiest days of my life. (*Pauses.*) Do you remember?

BETTY: How could I forget? You acted like a little boy.

GEORGE: I got it all, the new boat smell and the new shiny look and the prospect of hours of fishin', water skiin', and explorin' the bayous with you and the boys. I thought the boat was goin' help strengthen the family and our marriage. I thought it would bring us happiness.

BETTY: And the reality?

GEORGE: You know what happened! The kids didn't want to come with me. They didn't give a hoot about a bass boat or bondin' with their dad. They were just as happy ridin' their bikes around the neighborhood or spendin' an all-nighter playing video games with their friends. You sure as hell didn't wanna go, especially with all the studyin' and workin' you were doin'. I hated fishin' alone. And then there was the insurance, the fishin' license, the gas, the dockin' fees, the landin' fees and the boat payments. It cost a fortune! Every year, more money, more work, more effort, just to keep the thing afloat. And for what?

BETTY: (*Gives GEORGE a back rub.*) Settle down. (*Pauses.*) Just sell the boat for whatever you can get so at least we won't default on the payments and ruin our credit rating.

GEORGE: An ad in the newspaper costs $600 a week, not countin' the weekends. I won't have any money comin' in besides unemployment, remember? We can't touch the 401K. That would be terrible.

BETTY: You're right about that. For heaven's sake, don't touch your retirement. But I can find the money for the ad. I've squirreled some money away.

GEORGE: Yeah, I forgot that you have a real job now, a real salary, and a better one than me after your four years of community college. I got it. You're the smart one now, the one with a stable job and a stable income. Don't remind me!

BETTY: (*Tries to comfort GEORGE.*) You helped me during my four years in school. I just got lucky, that's all. I was in the right place at the right time.

GEORGE: Lucky? (*Pushes her away.*) You were smart and I was dumb. You saw the handwritin' on the wall and got an education and got into the medical field. Meanwhile, I just waited and watched as three plants closed and consolidated, one after another.

BETTY: Don't be ridiculous. You're smarter than I ever was.

GEORGE: Really? I've got a pink slip (*flashes it in the air*) and a bass boat that I don't need or want any more. I'm still payin' for that Goddamn thing that we hardly ever used. (*Grabs BETTY.*) Do you really want to be associated with such a bass boat ownin' loser like me?

BETTY: I never said that!

GEORGE: But you think it, don't you?

BETTY: No!

GEORGE: (*Shakes BETTY.*) Don't lie to me! The kids have heard you say it behind my back. They told me so.

BETTY: It's not true! They're just being malicious college kids. They don't know what they're saying most of the time.

GEORGE: Oh yes, rub that in while you're at it. We'll have three college graduates in the family and then me, a guy with a piece of shit GED and a pink slip. (*Shakes it in the air. Pauses.*) You told me so! Four years ago, you told me about Mr. Thor-o livin' in a cabin by a pond who said "people were rich in pro-por-tion to the things they did not own." I remember every word you said. I wondered about those words for four years now, so they're etched in my brain. (*Points to his skull.*)

BETTY: How do you remember that?

GEORGE: Because I thought you were talking about some hippy loser like Kaczynski the Unabomber. But you said Thor-o was a regular American phil-o-so-pher, and a pacifist and I don't know what else. I'd never heard of the guy, but I sure as hell didn't forget what you told me he said. I may not be that smart, but I got a good memory. You warned me and I wouldn't listen. You and Mr. Thor-o were both right. (*Pauses. Grabs a coat. Starts to leave.*) I'm leavin'.

BETTY: Where?

GEORGE: I don't know. Maybe offshore, maybe North Dakota, maybe Nigeria. Maybe the Middle East. Anyplace I can land a decent job.

BETTY: You're too old. They want young men, not middle-aged guys with health issues.

GEORGE: (*Raises his hand.*) Shut up! I ain't that sick.

BETTY: I'm taking about your blood pressure and your diabetes.

GEORGE: Yeah, and why not throw in my ED while you're at it. E-rec-tile dys-function, what a bunch of crap! I can't get it up or keep it up, just like I can't hold a job and can't pay the bills. I am a loser. You don't even have to say it.

BETTY: (*Sits down.*) Go then! Get out and stop whining. You're acting like a petulant child.

GEORGE: Pet-u-lant, eh? I guess that means like a spoiled brat?

BETTY: Sort of.

GEORGE: I guess that's another Thor-o word, eh?

BETTY: No.

GEORGE: Who then? Who said it, Mrs. Smart-ass book learner? (*Pauses.*) I should've never let you go back to college. I should've kept you barefoot and pregnant in the kitchen. I had my doubts back then and just couldn't see what good would come of it. All your workin' and studyin' and time and effort taken away from me and the kids. Now I know what happened. Now I see.

BETTY: Yes, you hesitated back then, but you let me go to school and I was grateful. And I kept a part time job, and studied, and took care of you and the kids. And yes, I was exhausted and fell asleep at night, but I still had time for the cooking and cleaning and everything else you asked me to do, even sex. (*Pauses.*) And while you were on me, all hot and sweaty and huffing and puffing, all I could think about was my next exam.

GEORGE: How romantic! So I forced you to have sex, back when I could perform, of course. That very upliftin'. (*Pauses.*) And who in hell could perform if you were thinkin' about your exam. You don't think a guy can feel that sorta thing? An uninterested woman is a real turn-off. Maybe I don't have e-rec-tile dys-function, maybe I just have frigid wife dys-function?

BETTY: That's mean-spirited. Don't blame me for your shortcomings. (*Pauses.*) And don't forget that I co-signed that boat loan even though I didn't really want to buy it.

GEORGE: I remember you threatenin' not to sign at the time. That was real mean-spirited back then and it's mean spirited now to bring it up.

BETTY: That's a lie! I just questioned the wisdom of a five-year loan for something that we didn't need and I didn't want. But you said it would be fine and I trusted so, I co-signed. (*Pauses.*) And now it's not fine!

GEORGE: No, it's not fine. You were right. You're always right. Cut off my balls and be done with it. I really do need to get outta here and just go somewhere else. (*Starts again to leave.*)

BETTY: Fine! So you will be somewhere else and you will still be unemployed and resentful and still own a damn bass boat. So who is going to pay the bills? Who is going to keep food on the table and a roof over our heads when your unemployment checks run out? Going somewhere else is not going to change anything. You'll just take your problems with you and start again.

GEORGE: (*Stops and turns.*) Did Thor-o say that, too?

BETTY: No, I did. All by myself.

GEORGE: (*Sighs. Looks defeated. Throws down his jacket and sinks down in a chair or sofa.*) I'm sorry, honey. I'm really proud of you. I'm proud of what you've accomplished and I'm proud you were the role model the kids needed for schoolin'. (*Takes BETTY's hand.*) I'm sorry. I just lost it. (*Pauses.*) Can I stay? At least until I can find somethin' else to do.

BETTY: (*Sits down next to GEORGE.*) Of course you can stay. This is your home, our home. (*Pulls out a school catalog.*) Maybe we can find something in here you could learn. Technician? IT specialist? Teacher, maybe?

GEORGE: (*Takes the book and flips through it.*) Algebra, biology, English, botany, computer science, forestry. (*Sighs.*) I'm not sure I'm smart enough for any of this. (*Looks at BETTY.*) You did it, but I'm not sure I could do it anymore. My mind just isn't as sharp as it used to be.

BETTY: Sure you could! It just takes time and you won't have to work. I can take care of the bills for a while. The kids are out of the house and they won't bother you.

GEORGE: I might be able to get somethin' part-time, like you did.

BETTY: That'll just be a distraction. You should concentrate on your studies. I can help you to learn. It'll be fun. Sort of like bass fishing, but with books.

GEORGE: (*Hugs BETTY.*) I don't deserve you, but I sure as hell need you.

BETTY: More than a bass boat?

GEORGE: God, yes! (*Holds BETTY's hand.*) I thought that when I bought that boat, it was the happiest day in my life. I really did. (*Pauses.*) I didn't think sellin' it would come anywhere close, but it's gonna be the second happiest.

BETTY: And getting married? Or having the boys? What about those days?

GEORGE: Of course, those were important, too. (*Sighs.*) I guess sellin' the bass boat drops to fifth and sixth or even lower after marryin' you and havin' the boys. (*Looks at BETTY.*) Better?

BETTY: Much better. (*Takes GEORGE by the shoulder.*) Now let's see when you can get started. And let's get that ad in the paper before the weekend. There's got to be somebody out there who wants a used bass boat, real cheap.

GEORGE: Yeah, I guess a fool's born every day. I bet Mr. Thor-o said somethin' about that.

BETTY: (*Shrugs.*) I don't think so, but P.T. Barnum said, "There's a sucker born every minute." We just have to find one to buy your bass boat.

(*BETTY and GEORGE laugh and exit. Lights dim to dark.*)

THE END

ALLERGIC TO SEAFOOD

CAST OF CHARACTERS

ELIZABETH THOMPSON: A flamboyant artistic woman in her mid-forties. Speaks with a very slight Southern accent.

BRIAN THOMPSON: Speaks with a marked Southern accent. A friendly, guileless fellow with no pretention.

GEORGE CARLYLE: A visiting professor of English from London. He speaks with a marked British accent and exudes self-assurance and self-sufficiency.

SETTING

A simple set with a couch, a couple of chairs and a coffee table. There can be some big coffee table books and perhaps an artsy knick-knack or two. If possible, there should be an oriental carpet.

BRIAN: (*Hands her some crackers.*) Here are the crackers you needed. (*Sniffs.*) Gosh, Lizzie, it smells like the Commander's Palace here.

ELIZABETH: (*Takes the crackers and puts them on the table in a bowl on the coffee table.*) I just whipped together something very down home, a Louisiana style seafood dinner: an appetizer of Gulf crab spread, followed by shrimp bisque, and then some crawfish *etouffée*. Dessert will be fresh raspberries over lemon sorbet, with a topping of Belgian chocolate and fresh whipped cream. The wine will be a lightly chilled California chardonnay, followed by Hungarian Tokay with the dessert. One of my friends brought me some Dutch coffee, which I've saved in the freezer for a special occasion. And that occasion is definitely now.

BRIAN: Wow! (*Tries to approach ELIZABETH, but she pushed him away.*) That sounds terrific. I'm not sure George really expects that much. He's really a pretty simple guy.

ELIZABETH: Simple! Look who's talking! Baseball, beer and fried chicken's good for you, but George is a sophisticated intellectual. Don't you remember those lovely evenings with George talking about art, literature, theater and dance? Didn't you get a tingle in your spine just listening to the witty exchanges with all those sensual British accents?

BRIAN: Yes, very sensual, now can I steal a kiss from the cook?

ELIZABETH: No, no, no! Not before you are as clean and spotless as this house. (*Eyes BRIAN's clothes and notices his aqua blue flip-flops*). Just go back and put on your loafers with tan socks, not white ones, and you'll be perfect.

BRIAN: Perfection is for God, remember, not for man.

ELIZABETH: Yeah, yeah. But it was perfect in London. You remember Piccadilly Circus and the Tate Gallery and the wonderful nights of theater, ballet and opera. (*Frowns.*) And here, it's so dismal and isolated.

BRIAN: Yep, nothing but swamps, alligators, and mosquitoes all around. (*Laughs.*) But it's home, and I'm glad to be here. Too much traffic in London for my liking. Give me that fried chicken, cold American beer, and a good baseball game, just like you said.

> (*Doorbell rings and ELIZABETH lets GEORGE in. GEORGE is dressed in a baggy sweater, rumpled pants, and Birkenstock sandals.*)

GEORGE: (*Holds a bottle of wine and small bouquet of flowers, both with prominent price tags still on them.*) For the charming hostess, with my compliments.

ELIZABETH: (*Places both the wine and flowers on the table. Scratches off the price tags.*) What a lovely gestures.

GEORGE: It was nothing, really.

BRIAN: (*Shakes hands. Gestures to the couch.*) Come in. Sit down. Make yourself comfortable.

GEORGE: Comfort, ah yes. That's a very relative notion down here. This area looked so looked so pleasant and lush flying in from the air. But once that airplane door opened, I felt like I was suffocating from this heat and humidity. You need scuba gear just to breathe in this place.

ELIZABETH: Well, at least it's air conditioned here. You'll be a lot more comfortable in just a minute.

GEORGE: It's positively frigid in here. From sauna to bloody fridge, how curious. Don't you have anything in-between?

ELIZABETH: (*To BRIAN.*) Go turn down the thermostat.

BRIAN: (*Adjusts the thermostat.*) That should be better, soon.

GEORGE: (*Looks around the room before picking out one of the chairs.*) I'm so glad to finally make it over to your home. It's been almost a month since I've been here on this exchange, but things have been hectic. This has not been a particularly easy transition for me. Lizzie already warned me that Central Louisiana is not what I have been used to in London. Even so, I hoped this so-called academic exchange, lopsided as it is, might still be interesting. You never know what you can unearth in such unlikely places.

BRIAN: Some of the students here are very good, even if there is a certain level of cultural illiteracy, even among college students.

GEORGE: Cultural illiteracy! It's astonishing. At first I thought it was a joke, but realized that it wasn't.

ELIZABETH: I wish it were a joke.

GEORGE: When I asked one of your students about Shaw, he said that it was a construction company based in Baton Rouge. (*Snorts with laughter.*) And then I said, no, no, we're talking about George Bernard, and another student tells me that's the mayor of Marksville, Louisiana. (*Snorts again.*)

ELIZABETH: (*Moves a bowl forward on the coffee table.*) Gulf crab spread with fresh dill. I hope you like it.

GEORGE: (*Looks at the plate.*) Very attractive, but I'm allergic to seafood.

BRIAN: (*Jumps up.*) What about something to drink?

ELIZABETH: All seafood?

GEORGE: Oh yes, crab, shrimp, and even those beastly little creatures you call crawfish. (*Pauses.*) Someone told me people around here sucked their heads. Can you imagine? The thought of such a perverse activity nauseates me. (*Pauses.*) Do you have any martini?

BRIAN: (*Looks at ELIZABETH.*) Do you know how to make a martini?

ELIZABETH: (*Shakes her head.*) We don't even have martini glasses.

GEORGE: (*Snorts again.*) Not that kind of martini! I mean the brand, Martini Rossi. It's a dark, sweet Vermouth, a very popular *apéritif* on the Continent. You know, a before dinner drink to open the appetite as the French say.

ELIZABETH: I'm afraid we don't have any. I don't even know if it's available locally.

GEORGE: Sure it is. I saw it at that horrible Piggly-Wiggly place down the road. You know, the supermarket that smells like moldy fruit and urine, a bit like my university assigned apartment, if I do say so myself. (*Snorts again, projecting a small chunk of snot onto their glass topped coffee table. Leans forward and wipes it up with a cocktail napkin.*) Sorry, dear, I sometimes just get carried away.

BRIAN: The Piggly-Wiggly is just a mile away. I can go pick some up now. It'll just take a few minutes.

GEORGE: Really, don't bother on my account. I can survive without it. Please don't go to any trouble on my account.

ELIZABETH: (*Jabs BRIAN in the ribs with her elbow.*) No, we insist!

BRIAN: It's not a bother! It's just down the street. (*Takes his keys.*) I don't want you to think we are country hicks. I'll be right back.

ELIZABETH: And don't forget to pick up the take out we ordered from the Chinese restaurant on the way back. It should be ready by now.

BRIAN: Chinese?

ELIZABETH: Yes, Chinese! (*To GEORGE.*) You do eat Chinese food, don't you?

GEORGE: Of course, I love it as long as they don't go too heavily with the monosodium glutamate. (*Watches BRIAN leave and then glances around the room at the books and artwork.*) Attractive library. (*Reaches for a cracker.*) I miss mine. I have those first editions of Oscar Wilde and Beardsley. The university library here doesn't even have a complete collection of T.S. Elliott and nothing by C.S. Lewis. Can you imagine? It's astonishing. What exactly are the students expected to learn here?

ELIZABETH: (*Opens her mouth. Nothing comes out. Shrugs her shoulders.*) Nothing, I guess.

GEORGE: My feeling, exactly! I was sort of hoping to glean something from this place. In theory it sounded interesting, an academic exchange to the hinterland of Louisiana. But it has just been an exhausting exercise in giving, giving, and giving, while getting nothing in return. I feel positively sucked dry, like a man covered with leeches. (*Pauses.*) I'm sure you can relate.

ELIZABETH: I sometimes feel like that, too. Mostly I just feel like this town doesn't understand me. When we were in London, I felt so alive, so invigorated, so in touch. I could have stayed there forever soaking up the culture. And then, of course, we met you and your fantastic circle of literary friends. It was like heaven, full of art, witty conversation, extraordinary creative people. I could have stayed there forever if Brian didn't have to come back here to teach.

GEORGE: (*Pulls a package out of his shirt pocket.*) I saw you admiring it in London. I knew it might be just the thing to brighten up your day.

ELIZABETH: (*Opens the small package.*) It's the sketch of Francis Bacon by his lover. It's gorgeous. You really shouldn't have. (*Bends over and kisses him and then backs away, surprised at herself.*)

GEORGE: I got it for a song at a second hand shop down in Chelsea. The owner didn't know what it was, of course, but I certainly did. (*Leans closer.*) I understand you, Lizzie. I saw it when you were in London. You are so full of vitality and curiosity. In fact, the thought of you was the only thing that really enticed me to come to this desolate place in the first place. (*Reaches forward and places his hand on ELIZABETH's knee.*) What exactly is an intelligent, sensitive, artistic soul like you doing in a place like this? How do you survive in this cultural vacuum?

ELIZABETH: (*Pants but remains motionless.*) I sometimes don't know myself. (*Looks at the picture.*) What can I possibly do to repay you?

GEORGE: (*His hand advances a couple of inches up her thigh.*) You could start by dropping by that little hellhole of an apartment of mine and giving me a real taste of Southern hospitality. (*Licks his lips.*) That might cheer me up a little.

ELIZABETH: (*Breathes heavily.*) I loved London. I loved the big city. I loved the way you spoke and moved and effortlessly flowed from one subject to the next, a well of knowledge, deep and appealing. Yes, I loved our stay in London.

GEORGE: And did you love me? (*Moves closer.*) I could see it in your eyes, the way your body moved, closer and closer to me. I could see the hungry flirtation in your eyes. Why do you think I came here? For the privilege of teaching ignorant coeds with Southern drawls about world-class literature? No, a thousand times no! Now is your chance to leave this life behind and taste the wonders of passion in a passionate place, not this wretched wasteland. (*Gestures around the room.*)

ELIZABETH: I do hate this place sometimes, but I can't throw my life here away. I'm married. I love Brian.

BRIAN: With his toothy grin and his pickup truck, his guns and baseball? How could you sink that low?

> (*BRIAN leans forward to kiss ELIZABETH on the mouth. ELIZABETH gasps, rising from her chair, and knocking the bowl of crab spread onto the floor. GEORGE leans forward to pick up the bowl, putting his head in the right position to receive the hardest slap that ELIZABETH can deliver.*)

ELIZABETH: You stupid, philandering prick! I love my husband and I love this place and I'd sooner die that get in bed with you! And besides,

I'm Baptist. Get out of my house! (*Grabs the flowers and bottle of wine and shoves them in his direction.*) And take your cheap wine and flowers with you! (*Give him the gift.*) And I don't want your gift either!

(*GEORGE reaches forward and takes the bottle, the flowers and the gift and goes to the door. ELIZABETH opens the door.*)

ELIZABETH: And don't bother coming back . . . ever!

(*GEORGE opens his mouth as if to say some final witty remark, but closes it with a slow movement that ends in an unflattering frown. Nods, turns and exits. ELIZABETH sits in the living room a few minutes before cleaning up the spilled crab spread. ELIZABETH goes to the kitchen and returns with two glasses of wine. BRIAN enters brandishing a bottle of Martini and Rossi Vermouth and a bag of Chinese food.*)

BRIAN: Got it! Martini-Rossi, fried rice and tiny spicy chicken. Nothing with seafood. (*Scans the room and looks down at ELIZABETH and the spilled food on the carpet.*) What happened? Where's George? Is he in the bathroom?

ELIZABETH: (*Shakes her head.*) He's gone.

BRIAN: Why?

ELIZABETH: (*Shrugs.*) Allergic to seafood. (*Stands and gives BRIAN a kiss and a hug.*)

BRIAN: What's that for?

ELIZABETH: Just for the heck of it. (*Pauses.*) How about some crab dip, shrimp bisque and crawfish étouffée?

BRIAN: I'd love it! And the Chinese food? (*Holds up the bag.*)

ELIZABETH: Stuff it in the fridge and we'll have it tomorrow. I'm in the mood for seafood.

(BRIAN and ELIZABETH leave the stage arm in arm. Lights dim to dark.)

THE END

THE COLFAX MASSACRE

CAST OF CHARACTERS

YOLANDA LACOUR: Creole woman of Cane River ancestry, born and raised in Oakland, California. She is dressed in something ostentatious, perhaps an African print dress. She speaks loudly and with authority. A trace of a black, Southern accent.

MAYOR BILLY CRAWFORD: African-American mayor of Colfax, Louisiana. He has a very pronounced rural black accent.

STEVE HEBERT: National Park Service employee. He should be dressed in a green shirt with a patch, denoting his official status. No particular accent.

DOROTHY MCCANN: Owner of the River Bend Plantation and descendant of General Elijah McCann, Confederate Civil War hero. She is prim and proper. She speaks with a thick Southern accent and is a member of the Daughters of the Confederacy and President of the Grant Parish Historical Society.

SETTING

Mrs. McCann's parlor. It has some period furniture and perhaps a Persian carpet. There is a very prominent painting of General Elijah McCann in his Confederate uniform hanging in the center of the rear wall, dominating the room. It should be lit by a spotlight, which can be turned off in the end. The four characters are already on the scene and seated in chairs in an open circle. There is a small table with some petit-fours on a tray.)

YOLANDA: Riot my ass! It was nothing but a vulgar massacre. (*Stands and gestures.*) Over 300 black militiamen were slaughtered in one day just when they were trying to surrender to the whites.

STEVE: Mrs. LaCour, we are working on the wording for the new historical marker. This is certainly the opportunity to correct the inaccuracies of the previous marker and set the historical record straight.

MAYOR: That's if we can ever figure out the funding. (*Leans toward DOROTHY and points to a plate of cakes.*) Miss Dorothy, could I please have one of those little cakes. They look mighty tasty. "Petit fours," I believe. (*Pronounces correctly in the French manner, "petti foor."*)

DOROTHY: (*Hands him the plate.*) But of course, Mayor. But they are really called *petit fours*, from the French. (*Pronounces à l'américain, "Petty Fours."*) I made them myself.

MAYOR: (*Eats the cake.*) Mighty tasty, indeed, however they're pronounced. (*Wipes his mouth.*) This interpretive center doesn't seem to be a high priority for the local civic leaders. (*Inclines in DOROTHY's direction.*) In fact, we can't really get anyone in the historical society interested besides Miss Dorothy here. And she's been kind enough to allow us to discuss the matter in her lovely home.

DOROTHY: And why should it be a priority? We have a perfectly fine historical marker that has designating the spot of that tragic event for the last 40 years. Speaking as the current President of the Grant Parish Historical Society, we are committed to the preservation of our common history and always have been.

YOLANDA: (*Jumps up.*) Whose history? Yours or the 300 dead black souls buried somewhere out here under the parking lot of the courthouse?

DOROTHY: All of our histories, of course. (*Pauses.*) And I might add that not a single one of my ancestors was involved in the sad events of

Easter, 1873. General Elijah McCann, (*indicates the portrait in back of her*) had been killed at the glorious Battle of Mansfield a decade earlier and his son, my great-great grandfather, was too young to have participated.

YOLANDA: Glorious Battle of Mansfield? Yes, indeed, those Confederates drove the Yankees out and then re-occupied Alexandria, or at least what was left of it after the fire.

DOROTHY: Set by that the Yankees, I might add, under the command of that malicious carpetbagger General Banks.

YOLANDA: Yes, so they say. But I hear it was the poor rednecks from surrounding communities, like this place, that came into Alexandria and looted what was left after the fire. They hated those rich town folks who had given General Banks such a warm, Southern welcome on his way through. Maybe some of your ancestors had a hand in that, too?

STEVE: Ladies, ladies, please. The historical record is bit fuzzy about all the circumstances of the burning of Alexandria. But it is much more accurate about the Colfax Massacre and that's what we're hear to discuss.

DOROTHY: Colfax riot, just like it says on the historical marker.

YOLANDA: Colfax massacre!

MAYOR: It's all old history, anyway. (*Takes another petit four.*) I'm just hopin' this interpretive center can bring some tourists and their money into this town. Historical tourism has lots of economic potential. It's eco-friendly and educational, a win-win for everyone. So ladies, can we hold down the bickerin' and just get along for a while?

YOLANDA and DOROTHY: (*Both shout at him simultaneously.*) NO!

YOLANDA: Not as long as descendants of slave owners write the history books and make the historical markers to commemorate their dead, not ours.

STEVE: That's the whole point. We want to incorporate the old marker, with its reference to the Colfax Riot, into the exhibit as an example of the change in historical perspectives from the time of its creation until our own. We need to put the former marker in the context of a more balanced and accurate historical record. (*Pauses.*) That's why we want the community, all of the community, blacks and whites, behind this effort.

YOLANDA: Look at her! (*Points to DOROTHY.*) She still sits there under the portrait of her Confederate slave-owner ancestor and clings to a past that's as dead and gone as him and the 300 poor blacks folks buried someplace under our feet.

DOROTHY: And the three whites that were killed, too, I might add. (*Pauses.*) Besides, your ancestors and mine both toiled on this land together and are they are all buried in our same sacred Southern soil.

YOLANDA: No! My people worked this land while your people drank mint juleps on their verandas and screwed black women in the back of the big house. (*Points off stage.*) Probably right in that back bedroom of this very same house! (*Stands and shows herself off.*) Why do you think I'm so white? Why do you think all of my people who still live up on the Cane River are so white? (*Points to the MAYOR.*) And why do you think the mayor is so black? (*Pauses.*) No offense intended.

MAYOR: None taken. (*To YOLANDA.*) However, I must ask you to calm down, Miss Yolanda. We have come a very long way since those sad times. I'd like to think of things in economic terms, not racial ones. That being said, I'm the first black mayor in this town since Reconstruction. And that's really say somethin' for around here.

YOLANDA: Yes, Reconstruction that died right here in Colfax and was buried by the Supreme Court in Washington, D.C. Those fools in the highest court of the land sent the white murderers back to Louisiana to be tried in state courts by all white racist jurors. Reconstruction died and civil rights with it for the next 100 years. Yes, that's what happened here in Colfax in 1873! (*To Dorothy pointing her finger.*) And don't you dare call it a riot when it was a black massacre!

STEVE: (*Jumps up. Gets between YOLANDA and DOROTHY.*) And that's precisely why we are interested in this new interpretive center. That's what we hope to emphasize in the lovely re-modeled bank building, the complex history of the area and the national significance of the tragic events of 1873 and their judicial implications.

YOLANDA: (*Not calming down.*) A hundred years! It took another hundred years to slog through this kind of racist crap. (*Points to the portrait.*) He might as well be wearing a white sheet, or maybe his son did. Maybe there are some white Klan costumes in the closets in this very house, in some armoire next to the bed where the white masters were screwing the black women, slave or otherwise.

DOROTHY: (*Jumps up.*) That's enough, young lady! You are insulting me in my own home and you know it. General McCann fought for his country, his beliefs and his family. He gave the last measure of his devotion to fight against Yankee invaders, bent on destroying his homeland and his way of life. As a Daughter of the Confederacy, I honor him and all the other patriots who died trying to preserve their freedom.

YOLANDA: And someone else's slavery!

DOROTHY: No, not slavery, but freedom based on states' rights!

YOLANDA: (*To STEVE and the MAYOR.*) States' right. It's incredible. You and your kind are still fighting the Civil War, over and over again, day after day, and year after year. (*Gets up into DOROTHY's face.*) You lost the Civil War, you bitch! (*Points to the MAYOR.*) There's a black president in Washington D.C., and here in the god-forsaken town, you have a black mayor, and a majority black city council in a majority black town. And there WILL be a truthful re-telling of this massacre in this new interpretive center as God is my witness!

STEVE: (*Calmly.*) I don't think you need to be evoking God in this. We just need to focus on the project, a nice refurbished bank building housing a wonderful collection of local artifacts, black, white and creole. (*Stands and becomes demonstrative.*) Can't you see it now? The mayor gives a speech when we cut the red ribbon. The press is there and takes pictures that show up in newspapers and television spots all over the country. Tourists will come flocking to see where history was made. We'll have books available, written about the incident and its national implications.

MAYOR: It think it sounds terrific, a joint local and federally funded project in the best interests of the community, the state and the nation. Everyone says it's all about collaboration and partnerships, workin' together in the best interests of the citizens. And all those tourist dollars flowing in will be an added bonus to everyone.

YOLANDA: (*Sits down.*) Yes, it sounds terrific. But will it ever happen while the cult of the glorious Confederate dead still lives in the hearts and minds of certain locals? (*Indicates DOROTHY.*)

DOROTHY: Where well it should live! (*Pauses.*) You can honor your dead while I honor mine.

YOLANDA: Well, at least you have headstones in your cemetery for the whites and even a phallic obelisk to the three glorious white people killed in the assault on the courthouse. They didn't' even die in combat, their cannon exploded.

DOROTHY: And a wreath is placed there at the monument every Easter in their memories.

YOLANDA: And the 300 blacks in the mass grave, wherever it is? There's no stone, no monument, just that racist so-called historical marker. (*Pauses.*) It's got to go! And it will even if I have to dig it out of the earth with my bleeding fingers. It has got to onto the trash bin of history where it belongs with all the Klan paraphernalia in this house and portraits of the glorious confederate dead. (*Jumps up and grabs the portrait of General McCann and tried to pull it off the wall.*)

DOROTHY: Stop! (*Jumps up and grabs YOLANDA's hands.*) Don't' you dare touch that, you impudent, black California troublemaker! Take your rabblerousing hands off that sacred image!

(*DOROTHY and YOLANDA tussle and come to blows, falling to the ground in the process. With difficulty, the MAYOR and STEVE pull them apart. The portrait hangs at an angle.*)

MAYOR: Settle down Miss Dorothy. I've never known you to raise your hand against any person in this town, black or white. You're a lady, remember. (*Pushes DOROTHY to a chair.*) Now you just sit down here and calm yourself down. Violence never solved any problems around here in the past and it's not goin' solve any now. (*Grabs a petit four and presents the plate to DOROTHY.*) A petit four, perhaps?

DOROTHY: No! I've lost my appetite.

STEVE: (*Pulls YOLANDA back and forces her into a chair.*) Sit down, Miss LaCour, please. Just sit down before you fall and break something.

(*STEVE and the MAYOR position themselves between the women.*)

STEVE: Mayor, this will be a big boon to your town. This on-going debate (*points to DOROTHY and YOLANDA*) reflects a lot of passion that we need to channel into the completion of this excellent project, not into bickering.

MAYOR: I hear you, loud and clear. We gotta have some other reason for folks to come to Colfax besides the Pecan Festival and Mudfest. (*Pauses.*) Although they're both pretty successful, I must say. But not a lot of high-end tourists come to them, at least not the ones interested in history and all that. High-end tourists are the ones with money. This is about economic development for everyone in this area, blacks and whites.

STEVE: (*To YOLANDA.*) Yes, like the Mayor says, there are tourist dollars out there to be made for sure. And we can set the historical record straight. It's a win-win. Can you just start to forgive, but not necessarily forget?

MAYOR: (*To DOROTHY.*) Miss Dorothy, don't you want to show some of that real Southern hospitality to a stranger from another state in your home.

DOROTHY: But she is so offensive, so brassy and insulting. That's hard to stomach, even for a Southern lady. Besides, she's from California and that's almost a foreign country.

MAYOR: Come, come, Miss Dorothy, I'm countin' on you. Let bygones be bygones.

DOROTHY: Okay. I'll try, but I hope to get an apology.

YOLANDA: (*Arms crossed.*) Fat chance! (*Turns her back.*)

STEVE: (*To YOLANDA.*) What if I told you something that might help you see eye-to-eye.

151

YOLANDA: It had better be good.

STEVE: Besides being a National Park Ranger, I'm something of a genealogist on the side. You both might be interested in knowing that General McCann here (*Points to the portrait*) had a bit of a property as well as a love interest up there in the Cane River country near Melrose.

YOLANDA and DOROTHY: And?

STEVE: Apparently he had a mistress up their by the name of Clotide Denis Metoyer, one of the descendants of the former French base commandant in Natchitoches, Monsieur St. Denis de Juchereau.

YOLANDA: So?

STEVE: Well, she had a daughter that eventually married a Mr. Bertrand LaCour.

YOLANDA: (*Astonished.*) My great grandfather? That Bertrand LaCour?

STEVE: The same.

(*YOLANDA and DOROTHY look at each other in disbelief.*)

DOROTHY: I don't believe you.

STEVE: It's all in the courthouse records in Natchitoches, which survived the burnings of the Civil War. Wonderful historical record, and very precise, I might add.

DOROTHY: That makes us. . . .(*Stops.*)

YOLANDA: Relatives!

(DOROTHY and YOLANDA sit in stunned silence.)

DOROTHY: *(To YOLANDA.)* I'm sorry, I didn't have the right to insult a stranger in my home and certainly not a. . . .

YOLANDA: A relative. Oh my God! I'm related to slave owners.

STEVE: Yes.

YOLANDA: You're my second or third cousin, twice removed, or something like that.

STEVE: Yes, something like that.

(After another silence, YOLANDA and DOROTHY approach one another and embrace.)

YOLANDA: I'm sorry, too. I had no right to attack you in your own home. It was crude and thoughtless. And especially if we're. . . .

DOROTHY: Family.

STEVE: *(To the MAYOR.)* I guess we can move forward with this project of mutual interest. *(Shakes hands with the MAYOR.)*

MAYOR: Of course, I'm all for brotherly love and sisterly love, too.

STEVE: Ladies?

YOLANDA and DOROTHY: Okay.

STEVE: So I suppose everyone is happy now?

(No one answers, but the portrait of General McCann goes dark when the spotlight is turned off. Everyone turns to look at the portrait. Lights dim to dark.)

THE END

THE BEST PREDICTOR

CAST OF CHARACTERS

LAUREN HUNTER: Middle-aged woman, dressed in nice clothing for a dinner party. She speaks correctly and has a certain nobility.

SOPHIA: Mrs. Hunter's daughter, a more Bohemian, younger woman, in her early thirties. She dresses more casually. She is less formal in her speech and manners.

FATHER SAM: A Catholic priest, friend of the family. He can be very portly and is clearly a *bon vivant* despite his clerical attire.

CARTER COUILLION: Fiancé of Sophia and a well-known local cardiologist. He has no accent. Carter wears a blue blazer over a rumpled dark blue shirt, which hangs over a pair of faded blue jeans.

SETTING

There is a dinner table, set for an elegant dinner, around which the action takes place. Lauren and Sophia are in the room as the play begins.

LAUREN: (*Stands by the table and arranges some flowers.*) Don't you think it's a bit soon to get into another romantic relationship?

SOPHIA: No, it's been a year since Jim and I got divorced. That seems long enough to me. Besides, my biological clock is ticking away.

LAUREN: You're only thirty-two. That's not too old. Women now are having children into their forties.

SOPHIA: Forties! My God, if I wait until then, I'd be the oldest mother in kindergarten. (*Pauses.*) I know you think Carter's too old for me, but ten years is not that big of a difference. Besides, he's still very attractive and he is very well connected socially.

LAUREN: He's still your boss.

SOPHIA: (*Narrows her eyes and glares.*) He is NOT my boss!

LAUREN: Perhaps not directly, but you both work at the hospital and you are a hospital employee. That's not a situation of equality. (*Picks up a piece of silverware.*) Do you think it's polished enough?

SOPHIA: Of course, it looks fine. It's beautiful. The table's beautiful. And that's all you care about, external appearances. (*Clutches her heart.*) I'm looking for something beyond the external, something deeply personal and beautiful on the inside.

LAUREN: Like your previous husband, the one that abused you? That marriage didn't exactly work out, did it?

SOPHIA: Don't do that! As a social worker, you should know better than to humiliate a client by bringing up failed past relationships.

LAUREN: You are not a client. You are my daughter and you are also a very smart woman in every sense, except perhaps in your choice of men.

SOPHIA: I love Carter and Carter loves me.

LAUREN: Perhaps, but he comes with several grown children, an ex-wife, and . . . .(*Pauses.*)

SOPHIA: And what?

LAUREN: And a lot of money.

SOPHIA: Yes, he does make a lot of money and he slaves for every penny of it. I've never seen a man work harder in my life. He has thousands of clients and he works day and night.

LAUREN: Yes, he works day and night and weekends. But will he have time for you? (*Pauses. Goes to SOPHIA and embraces her.*) I don't want to see you hurt again. All those bruises and black eyes nearly killed me. I would as soon murder a man than let one do that to you again.

SOPHIA: Carter is not Jim! You've got to believe me!

LAUREN: (*Reaches up and grabs SOPHIA's hand.*) I want to believe you. I want you to be happy and independent. I want you to know the same happiness I knew with your father. (*Pauses.*) I really do.

SOPHIA: Then why don't you just let me go ahead and marry Carter and be happy?

LAUREN: Because I worry about you.

SOPHIA: Why? Why do you worry about me?

LAUREN: Because the best predictor of future behavior is past behavior.

SOPHIA: (*Pulls away from LAUREN.*) That's an insult and it's untrue. (*Turns to walk away.*) I'm going in the kitchen and help Father Sam. Thanks for the conversation. I hope you can be nicer when Carter arrives. (*Leaves and goes into the kitchen.*)

FATHER SAM: (*Comes in through the door as SOPHIA goes out. Surveys the table with satisfaction.*) It looks beautiful. It will be a perfect compliment to the food.

LAUREN: Thank you so much for helping. You're a real love. You know this is really important to Sophia. (*Changes tone.*) What exactly to you have planned in there?

FATHER SAM: Well, I have some *pâté de foie gras* on a bed of arugula, steak Teriyaki with baby potatoes and asparagus, and, for dessert, fresh raspberries on sorbet with fresh mint sprigs.

LAUREN: Yum! And the wine?

FATHER SAM: A 1984 *Côte de Bourg*, a superb Bordeaux from your late husband's well-furnished wine cellar.

LAUREN: Ah, yes, that was one of his favorites. Excellent choice on your part, of course. (*Looks at FATHER SAM.*) You are something: priest, cook, sommelier and heaven only knows what else. In any case, you're really an angel.

FATHER SAM: Far from it. Now let me get back into the kitchen and finish up a few things. Sophia's helping me. (*Looks at his watch.*) Dr. Couillon should be here anytime.

> (*FATHER SAM goes out. The doorbell rings and LAUREN goes to answer it. SOPHIA joins her from the kitchen and the two women go to the door. CARTER holds a bouquet of inexpensive looking flowers.*)

CARTER: Good evening, Mrs. Hunter. (*Presents the flowers to LAUREN.*) Here's something for you. (*Looks at SOPHIA and gives her a kiss on the cheek.*)

LAUREN: (*Takes the flowers and extends her hand to him.*) Thanks you so much, Dr. Couillon, they are beautiful.

CARTER: Beautiful flowers for a beautiful woman.

LAUREN : You are too kind. Come in.

FATHER SAM: (*Enters from kitchen dressed in a white apron over his priestly attire.*) And you must be Dr. Carter Couillon.

CARTER: Yes, and you are?

FATHER SAM: (*Wipes his hands on the apron.*) I'm so sorry. I'm Father Sam Bruschetti, Lauren's friend and the parish priest. At your service. (*Bows in CARTER's direction.*)

CARTER: (*To SOPHIA.*) Your mother has a priest for a cook?

LAUREN: Don't I wish. (*Points to FATHER SAM.*) Father Sam just loves to cook and he volunteered to help out in the kitchen.

FATHER SAM: (*To SOPHIA and CARTER.*) You're probably both starving. Would you like a before dinner drink?

SOPHIA: Mom, Carter has to go back to the hospital in a couple of hours. Could we skip the drinks and go straight to the dinner?

FATHER SAM: (*Looks at CARTER.*) Of course, I'm ready if you are. What do you say, Lauren?

LAUREN: The guest is always king. (*Indicates the table.*)

CARTER: Wow! This looks beautiful.

LAUREN: Thank you, I'll take that as a compliment. Now, please sit down where you name is located.

(*CARTER takes his place across the table from LAUREN. SOPHIA sits in front of FATHER SAM, who goes back into the kitchen, sheds his apron, and reappears with a tray with four glasses of white wine. Plates with the pâté de foie gras are already on the table at each place.)*

FATHER SAM: (*Passes out the glasses and sits down. Raises his glass.*) To friends, to family, to good food and good wine! *In vino veritas!*

(*ALL raise their glass and then drink.*)

CARTER: And a prayer? You're a real priest aren't you?

FATHER SAM: Of course. (*Bows his head.*) Bless this food to our use and us to your service. Amen.

ALL: Amen.

CARTER: (*Laughs.*) Pretty short prayer for a priest.

FATHER SAM: (*Turns to CARTER.*) Brevity is the soul of wit. So how exactly did you and Sophia meet?

CARTER: (*Answers with a mouthful of food.*) Sophia works at the hospital for one of my colleagues. (*Looks at SOPHIA.*) I've always had my eye on her. She's a real beauty, and really smart, too.

FATHER SAM: And what is your line of work?

CARTER: I'm an interventional cardiologist. I thought everyone around here knew me.

FATHER SAM: (*Shakes his head.*) I can't say I have. Nor have I seen you at Mass lately.

CARTER: Too busy saving lives, Padre. And I guess you haven't needed a heart cath yet either, even though I think you're working on it. (*Points*

FATHER SAM's protruding belly. Laughs a loud coarse laugh, projecting out bits of food as he does so.)

FATHER SAM: I guess you must be a free thinker?

CARTER: Nah, just too busy, mostly. I've got lives to save, money to make. Besides, even though I was raised a Catholic, I don't have much use for formal religion, if you know what I mean. (*Winks at FATHER SAM.*)

SOPHIA: No, what exactly do you mean?

CARTER: Well, we do so much free medical work that I think I'm already doing my part for charity. One third of folks don't pay their bills, especially those losers that end up in the ER with their heart attacks and no insurance. Those folks get everything free. You save souls while I save lives. I just get tired of those deadbeats that think it's their right to get excellent care, day and night and never pay a dime.

FATHER SAM: Dead beats?

CARTER: Yeah, the uninsured who eat and smoke themselves to death, but can't seem to ever have enough money to pay an insurance premium. They just show up in the ER as sick as dogs and then they'll sue you if everything doesn't come out perfectly.

SOPHIA: Aren't they supposed to come to the hospital when they're sick?

CARTER: Sure, but they used to go to the state run hospitals and get treated there for free. Now the law has changed and we can't refuse them. It's crazy. We end up writing off thousands of dollars every year. I have to work twice as hard just to earn the same amount of money I earned a few years ago.

FATHER SAM: Besides free care, do you give to any other charities?

CARTER: Other charities! My God, isn't that enough? Isn't getting up day and night while running the risk of being sued enough? At this rate, I'll be living in the poor house before you know it.

LAUREN: Poorhouse? I thought you had a lovely house on the lake. Something patterned after a French villa from the Riviera?

CARTER: That mausoleum! My first wife still lives there until she can dump that white elephant. Who in the heck needs 8,000 square feet of marble and granite? It's more like a hellhole than a house, especially with her still in it.

SOPHIA: Perhaps we can talk about something else?

> (*FATHER SAM takes plates and returns with a platter of steak strips. LAUREN serves the food while FATHER SAM pours the first taste of the Bordeaux to CARTER.*)

CARTER: (*Looks at the small amount in the glass.*) Hey, that's pretty cheap. Don't you even serve a full glass?

FATHER SAM: Cheap?

CARTER: I mean I know it's supposed to be good wine, but that's just a tiny swallow.

SOPHIA: (*Leans forward to CARTER.*) It's just for tasting, Carter, you're the guest of honor. You get to sample the wine.

CARTER: Oh yeah, guest of honor and all that. I get it. (*Swirls the glass and downs the contents with a quick swallow.*) Good, really good. Now you can serve a full glass, *garçon*. (*Laughs raucously and drinks.*) It's good, really good. (*Looks at the bottle. Pronounces the French with a*

163

bad American accent.) Côte de Bourg, 1984. *Ap-pel-la-tion Con-tro-lée.* Wow, I bet that put your dad back a few bucks. I was still a medical student then. (*Downs the glass in a few swallows and then takes the bottle and re-fills his glass to the brim.*) Yeah, this is really great stuff.

(*SOPHIA and LAUREN eat in silence. CARTER takes a few mouthfuls.*)

CARTER: Eh, Padre? How'd you learn how to cook so good?

FATHER SAM: First, the dinner is really the work of Mrs. Hunter. (*Indicates LAUREN.*) I only helped a little. Second, I was a professional cook when I got the calling.

CARTER: (*Laughs.*) From gourmet to God, that's a good one. (*Laughs again.*) This is really good meat. I bet it cost a bundle. (*Finishes off his second glass of wine and pours. Turns to LAUREN.*) You've got a great daughter here, Lauren. She's classy. I mean very classy. I never hear her swear and she never wears slutty clothes like some of those other girls around the hospital. She always does what she's asked to do and never rocks the boat. (*Takes several gulps of Bordeaux and refills his own glass to the brim.*) My first wife wouldn't do a damn thing I asked her to do. Spend, spend, spend, that's all she ever did. She'd even give money away to people: United Way, Red Cross, Doctors Without Borders, even Amnesty International of all ridiculous causes. She said we were blessed and I earned ten times the amount of everyone else in the state. (*Stuffs more food in his mouth and swishes it down with more wine. Speaks with his mouth full.*) What do I care about the United Way? You know what Jesus said, Padre? (*Does not wait for an answer.*) "The poor ye shall always have among you." We just got more of them around here than in most places, right?

FATHER SAM: (*Sighs.*) Yes, Jesus did say that, at least the first part. He also said that it was harder for a camel to pass through the eye of a needle than for a rich man to enter into the kingdom of heaven.

(*A silence follows. CARTER's mouth twitches at each corner before it opens wide in an explosion of laughter. As the laughter dies down, CARTER gasps three times before starting to choke on some food in his mouth. CARTER clutches his hands to his throat. His eyes and mouth open wide. A raspy squeaking comes out.*)

SOPHIA: He's dying! Do something!

FATHER SAM: (*Jumps up from his chair, hits the table and knocks over the bottle of wine. Runs in back of CARTER and grabs him around the gut. Does a Heimlich maneuver.*) One, two, three!

(*At the sound of three, FATHER SAM heaves CARTER up so strongly that CARTER rises from his chair. A mouthful of Teriyaki steak flies out of his mouth and lands on the table. CARTER gasps a few times before FATHER SAM lets him slump back into his chair. LAUREN and SOPHIA both rush up to either side CARTER, who looks at them.*)

CARTER: Christ, I almost died! (*Staggers to his feet and leans on the dining table.*) I could've died. (*Looks at SOPHIA.*) Your mom and her holy cook just about killed me. I could sue the hell out of them both. And I probably should. (*To SOPHIA.*) Come on, honey. We got to get out of here.

SOPHIA: (*Shakes her head.*) You go on. I'd rather stay. (*Pauses.*) I want to help clean up.

CARTER: (*Gives her an evil look.*) It's them or me? Your choice. If I leave without you, I'm not looking back.

SOPHIA: Yes, I know. It is my choice and I'm making it. I'm staying.

CARTER: Suit yourself! (*Grabs his jacket and stomps out, slamming the door.*)

165

(FATHER SAM, SOPHIA and LAUREN sit back down at the table. LAUREN looks at the spilled wine and the piece of meat, and covers it with a napkin. LAUREN begins to giggle and then laugh and FATHER SAM and SOPHIA join in. The laughter continues until they tire.)

FATHER SAM: (*Stands up.*) We have a lovely dessert of raspberry sorbet, topped with seasonal berries, and accompanied by coffee and Belgian chocolates. Anyone interested?

(SOPHIA and LAUREN raise their hands in unison.)

SOPHIA and LAUREN: Me! Me!

(Lights dim to dark.)

THE END

THE MANUSCRIPT

CAST OF CHARACTERS

JAKE: Amateur writer. Middle-aged. Casually dressed. No regional accent.

FRANK: Salesman from Perfect Self-Publishing House. Dressed in a suit. May have an Eastern accent (New York or New Jersey). He speaks fast. Younger than Jake.

CLARA: Jake's wife. A no-nonsense woman. May have an indefinable foreign accent or none at all. Casually dressed. Middle-aged but attractive.

SETTING

There are a couple of chairs and a coffee table. Jake and Frank are discussing around the table. There is a thick manuscript that is passed around during the play.

(*JAKE and FRANK are sitting on around the table. FRANK is handling the manuscript.*)

SCENE I: THE SALES PITCH

JAKE: So what do you think about it?

FRANK: As I told you on the phone, it's good. It's got a lot of potential.

JAKE: Do you think anyone will buy it?

FRANK: Sure! We just need to get it out there to the general public. Writers are discovered every day. You will need a publicist, and a commercial website, and a distribution network. (*Stands and hands the manuscript to JAKE.*) And we can arrange a speaking tour and book signings. There's even a screenplay symposium in Las Vegas. (*Waves his arms in the air.*) I can see it now, you sitting at a table with dozens of directors and producers looking at this manuscript. My friend, the sky's the limit!

JAKE: And how much will this all cost?

FRANK: Cost? What's cost when it's your career as a writer at stake? We have authors who were sitting at home undiscovered and now they're earning six figures in annual royalties.

JAKE: How many writers like that do you have?

FRANK: (*Pauses.*) Well, not many, but they are out there.

JAKE: One in a hundred? One in a thousand? Or one in a hundred thousand?

FRANK: It's no different than professional football. That's a one in a hundred thousand chance, too, but it does happen. It happens every day. Your literary work has real potential. I tell you it does, and I've seen thousands of them.

JAKE: Maybe, but how could it be improved to increase my chances of commercial success?

FRANK: (*Sits down and picks up the manuscript.*) Jake. May I call you Jake?

JAKE: Of course.

FRANK: I like you, Jake, so now I'm putting on my editorial hat, not my marketing one. (*Looks back at the manuscript.*) You're technically very good. You write well and you dream up the most fascinating situations, but it seems a bit short on real passion.

JAKE: Passion like sexual passion?

FRANK: No, I mean passion as in a truly engaged writer.

JAKE: I work hard at this! I'm passionate!

FRANK: Yes, I know and that's why I'm here. But it's not passion about doing the work, but passion about the subject. You have to care about the subject to infuse the characters with that *je ne sais quoi*. (*Pronounced "je ne say quah."*) (*Waves his hands in the air.*)

JAKE: I don't understand French; you'll have to translate.

FRANK: Sorry, I get carried away. (*Pauses.*) It's that something intangible, that indefinable quality of engagement, that impulsion that just cannot be denied. It's what it costs the writer in pain and suffering to create their *oeuvre*, (*pronounced "euv-rah."*) their body of work. (*Pauses.*) Readers know it when they read it. They can recognize it in the text by some mysterious communion of spirits. (*Pauses.*) If you don't care about your characters, why should the reader care about them either? Do you really care?

JAKE: (*With passion.*) I do care!

FRANK: About what? Politics? The national debt? Healthcare policy? Family values?

JAKE: Yes, all those things!

FRANK: Those are nothing but abstractions. The reader wants concrete connections between you and your flesh and blood characters. They want to care about your characters like you do. And then they want conflict, hope for change, and a dramatic arch where people really do change. They want to believe they can get out of their sordid, petty lives and fly on the wings of your imagination and your talent to places they have never been before.

JAKE: (*Grabs his manuscript.*) It's here! It's all here!

FRANK: (*Half-heartedly.*) Yes, some of it is there.

JAKE: But is it enough?

FRANK: (*Shrugs.*) That's why I'm just a marketer. Content's not really my thing.

JAKE: But you talk like an editor.

FRANK: I'm just a marketer, really.

JAKE: (*Flips through the manuscript.*) There's sensitivity here. I can feel it, because I put it there. You know and I know I have talent, sensitivity and perseverance and it's all in here.

FRANK: (*A bit embarrassed.*) Yes, of course. So let's get back to getting this work out there to the reading public, not writing the next great American novel. (*Shows a paper.*) So the publicist is $500, and the professional interactive website is $1,200 and the marketing materials and distribution are another $700.

JAKE: And the total is?

FRANK: Only $2,400. But since you are a previously published author, we can offer you a generous 25% discount for the next three days.

JAKE: Which makes it?

FRANK: Only $1,810, a real bargain.

JAKE: (*Looks at the paper.*) I'll have to ask my wife. She's the family accountant. (*Calls off stage.*) Clara! Clara! Can you come in here a minute?

FRANK: Does your wife write, too?

JAKE: Not that I know of, but she's a hell of a reader. Except for my works, of course. She refuses to read them.

FRANK: I understand. A prophet's never honored in his own country.

(*CLARA enters and stops in front of FRANK.*)

JAKE: (*Presents FRANK.*) This is Mr. Frank Levin from Perfect Self-Publishing House.

CLARA: Nice to meet you.

FRANK: (*Stands and takes CLARA's hand.*) Nice to meet you. I hear you're been a supportive wife to your husband's literary career.

CLARA: Well, you've heard wrong!

JAKE: Frank here is proposing a marketing package for my last book that includes a publicist, website and outreach campaign for only $2,400.

FRANK: But since Jake is an established author, there is a time-limited offer of 25% off.

CLARA: Which makes it?

JAKE and FRANK: Only $1,810.

CLARA: (*Laughs raucously.*) You've got to be kidding!

JAKE: No, and it's really a good deal.

CLARA: We have a leaking roof, a car that's falling apart, electrical problems and a daughter who needs money for college and you want to spend $1,810 on some vanity press marketing deal?

FRANK: That's harsh.

CLARA: Not as harsh as I'm going to be if you don't get out of here right away Mr. . . .what did you say your name was?

FRANK: Levin, Frank Levin.

CLARA: (*Points to the door.*) Mr. Levin, that's the way out!

JAKE: Can't we talk this over a few minutes?

CLARA: There's no more talking to be done. No, no, no and NO! That's my final answer.

FRANK: Your husband's work shows a great deal of talent and sophistication.

CLARA: And no one is interested, no even me!

FRANK: Surely a supportive wife such as yourself would not frustrate your husband's literary aspirations?

CLARA: Literary aspirations? Do you know how much this vanity money pit has already cost us? Five books and maybe he's received a $100 in cumulative royalties.

JAKE: (*Pouting.*) It's not about the money.

CLARA: What do you mean? (*To FRANK.*) It's all about the money that you disingenuous people are making off no-talent, self-deluded hacks.

FRANK and JAKE: Ouch!

CLARA: (*To JAKE.*) Look at this guy! (*Points to FRANK.*) That's his job to sell marketing packages to chumps like you. He doesn't care if you have talent or not, only if you have the money to spend and are willing to spend it.

FRANK: Madame, I'm a literary connoisseur and an art lover as well, not just a salesman.

CLARA: Don't Madame, me! I'm just one of the girls. (*To JAKE.*) And I hate what you write! It gives me the creeps. You steal people's lives and think it's clever. I hate every word. (*Brushes the manuscript to the floor. Softly.*) But I do love you as a person, as strange as that may sound . . .at least for now.

JAKE: You really hate what I write?

CLARA: Yes.

FRANK: Your husband is an undiscovered genius, a true original talent.

JAKE: (*To FRANK.*) Thank you.

FRANK: And as a testimony to my faith in his talent and literary future, I am prepared to offer you a 50% reduction off the original marking package price.

JAKE: Which means?

FRANK: An incredible $1,200 for the whole package, divided into four easy installments of $300.

JAKE: (*To CLARA.*) Honey, that's too good a deal to pass up, don't you think?

CLARA: No, I don't think! I know that it's a waste of your hard-earned money. (*Grabs the manuscript off the floor.*) This is hours of your life, slaving away on page after page of writing that no one wants to read for $1,200 or even $12,000. You can't even pay people to like your work. It doesn't matter to the people out there, Jake. You do have the passion, but you don't have enough talent. I'm sorry.

JAKE: But Frank here just said I needed more passion and that I did have the talent.

CLARA: (*Pauses. Moves next to FRANK.*) Give me your right hand. (*Pulls FRANK down on the sofa.*)

FRANK: (*Hesitates.*) Why?

CLARA: (*Assumes an ill-defined Eastern European Gypsy accent.*) I want to read your future.

FRANK: (*Gives CLARA his hand.*) Okay.

CLARA: (*Examines FRANK's hand.*) Your love life is here. I see that it has several breaks in it. You have been unlucky in love.

FRANK: Well, I am on my fourth marriage, at least for the time being.

CLARA: And this is your prosperity line. It's indistinct, weak, and also broken.

FRANK: I have had some economic reversals, although things are pretty good for the present.

CLARA: And this is your longevity line. It starts strong, and then fades and comes to an abrupt end here, where it crosses your destiny line.

FRANK: Is that bad?

CLARA: Yes, very bad. (*Pauses. Drops the assumed accent.*) And if you don't get out of my house this very minute, your lifeline will end here and now. (*Shows the door.*) Get out now, Mr. Levin, while you still can.

FRANK: (*To CLARA.*) You're good, very good. You have talent and passion. Have you ever considered working with Perfect Self-Publishing to write a manual on palm reading? We have an entire line of paranormal books that do very well.

CLARA: (*Reaches into a basket on the table.*) Would you like to see my gypsy grandmother's hunting knife? It's a real beauty.

FRANK: No, no. I think I need to get going. (*Exits hastily.*)

CLARA: (*Sighs.*) Jakey, Jakey, Jakey.

JAKE: $1,200 was a real deal.

CLARA: (*Hugs JAKE from behind the chair with her hands around his neck.*) You're a fine man, a good provider, and a faithful husband. (*Pretends to strangle JAKE.*) You're also so vain I could kill you if your vanity doesn't choke you first. I do still believe in you.

JAKE: (*Kisses CLARA.*) Thanks.

CLARA: (*Takes the manuscript.*) And I do believe in us, but not in this. (*Drops it on the table.*)

JAKE: (*Slumps down.*) All I need is just one Pulitzer Prize.

CLARA: Okay, and if you win a Pulitzer, you can buy a marketing program from Perfect Self-Publishing. Deal?

JAKE: Deal!

CLARA: By the way, did you see this letter?

JAKE: It's from that short story writing contest. (*Tears open the envelope. Reads.*)

CLARA: Good news?

JAKE: No, rejected again.

CLARA: (*Hugs JAKE.*) Perhaps your writing is rejected by those people, but you are not rejected from me, not from my heart. (*Puts her hands over her heart.*)

JAKE: So you really do love me? You're really passionate about me?

CLARA: Yes.

JAKE: That gives me an idea.

CLARA: Not stealing my life, are you?

JAKE: Nay, just borrowing. Want an ice cream cone?

CLARA: Sure.

JAKE: Chocolate or vanilla?

CLARA: Both!

(*Lights dim to dark.*)

SCENE II: LAS GRINGAS CON PLUMAS
(TEN MONTHS LATER)

(The same coffee table and a couple of chairs. JAKE is reading a letter.)

JAKE: Not again!

CLARA: What happened?

JAKE: My latest play's been rejected . . . again! (*Holds the rejection letter.*) I thought I had a good chance this year. I really worked on that manuscript. (*Pauses. Hands the letter to CLARA.*) Show's you how much I know.

CLARA: (*Puts the letter on the coffee table.*) I think you've probably made a lot of progress in your writing over the last year or so, really.

JAKE: So if I've made progress, why do I keep getting rejected year after year? I write, I re-write, I go to workshops, go to readings, and read books about writing. (*Pauses.*) And I just get rejected year after year, even from some rinky-dink local contest like this one.

CLARA: Just keep writing. Just keep plugging along. It takes time and work.

JAKE: Time, work and talent. (*Pauses.*) Maybe that's what I really do lack, talent.

CLARA: (*Cooly.*) We've already discussed that. Talent can be cultivated! It sometimes just takes time. And even if you may have improvements to make as a writer, your work product is very much appreciated at your firm. You're recognized as an important and creative member of the business team.

JAKE: Yes, a good guy at my job and as a loser writer. You've said as much to me in the past, a "no talent, self-deluded hack," remember?

CLARA: (*Angrily.*) Yes, spoken in a moment of anger. But who cares? Writing never paid any of our bills. Writing doesn't send our kids college. Writing doesn't bring you anything but grief. (*Goes to JAKE and puts her hands around his shoulders.*) Yes, I know writing is important to you. It would be nice to be accepted in this play contest, but it's not the end of the world if you don't write the great American novel or the great American play. How many *Death of a Salesman's* do we need, anyway? One is depressing enough.

JAKE: (*Slumps down in the sofa.*) I'm depressed. Profoundly depressed.

CLARA: Honey, not this again.

JAKE: I tell you, it's endogenous. It's in me and it's chemical.

CLARA: And treatable. (*Pauses.*) Don't let this writing stuff get you down like this. It's just not important. (*Pauses.*) No, let me rephrase that, it's important to you, but I don't value you any less whether you get a story or a play accepted or not. Maybe you have mastered the technical aspects of writing, but just need some more inspiration?

JAKE: From what? From whom?

CLARA: Anything you find passionate. Something you love. (*Shrugs.*) Me, for instance?

JAKE: (*Laughs.*) You inspire me everyday. But you're the bedrock of my life, that solid foundation on which everything else grows and flourishes.

CLARA: Bedrock, eh? Not too flattering. I don't know anything that grows on bedrock. (*Struts around in front of JAKE.*) And how about your muse? What about that? Do I count as your day-to-day inspiration?

JAKE: (*Ponders.*) You are my life, my wife, and the mother of our children. I adore you, of course. (*Pauses.*)

CLARA: But I don't inspire you, is that it?

JAKE: (*Sadly.*) No, not anymore.

CLARA: (*Sits down.*) And who or what does inspire you?

JAKE: (*Long pause. Looks imploringly at CLARA.*) Frank.

CLARA: (*Incredulous.*) What? Frank Levin, that Perfect Self-Publishing salesman?

JAKE: Yes, I think so?

CLARA: You think so?

JAKE: I'm pretty sure. (*Pauses.*) We've gotten to know one another very well over the Internet during the last ten months and for some reason he fascinates me. He's fairly young, handsome, articulate, uninhibited and. . . .

CLARA: And unmarried after his fourth wife?

JAKE: Yes, I think so. At least he's between marriages.

CLARA: And gay?

JAKE: No, I don't think so.

CLARA: You don't think so! Have you asked?

JAKE: No, of course not! That's personal.

CLARA: (*Laughs.*) I'd say so, but it's also pretty damn important. (*Pauses.*) So what exactly is the attraction? I thought he just wanted to sell things to you, some marketing packages and the like.

JAKE: In the beginning, yes, but now that I've gotten to know him better I find he exudes some sort of magnetism. He makes me feel good about my writing and myself. And everything he touches seems to grow and blossom. Besides being a successful salesman, he also writes, he paints, he dances and he's already published several books of his own.

CLARA: So?

JAKE: That's quite an accomplishment for young man.

CLARA: He's not that young, I tell you. Not if he's already been through a few marriages. Besides it's just self-publication, vanity press. That's meaningless. He probably gets some sort of half-off discount. By the way, don't you think I'm young, attractive and successful?

JAKE: Sure, but you're me wife.

CLARA: So?

JAKE: And after thirty years of marriage, it's like eating chicken every day, it just gets boring. Besides, neither of us is that young and attractive anymore.

CLARA: (*Angrily.*) So now I'm a tired old tasteless chicken breast?

JAKE: Breast? (*Sighs.*) If I were only so lucky.

CLARA: (*Furious.*) So maybe I'm just a thigh, or a neck or a tough old gizzard? (*Pauses.*) You're repulsive and insulting! How could I have put up with it for so long?

JAKE: No, it's not like that. I didn't mean it to by insulting.

CLARA: But it sure sounds that way. (*Shakes her finger.*) If you'd wanted beef or sushi, why didn't you just talk to me about it?

JAKE: I don't like sushi.

CLARA: I know that! It was just a figure of speech, for God's sake. Besides, what do you think I feel like? You've been less than potent for years now. Did I say anything? Did I complain that you couldn't perform? Did I make you rush out and get Viagra or Cialis or underarm testosterone? No! No! And NO! (*Pauses.*) You can be so self-centered it's pitiful. You're delusional and I'm just part of your fantasies, and a boring part at that. "Like eating chicken every day."

JAKE: I'm sorry. (*Tries to take CLARA in his arms.*)

CLARA: (*Pushes JAKE away.*) No! It's too late for that. This chicken thigh is finally flying the coop. (*Pulls out a letter.*) I had serious scruples about this, but now they're gone. Here's my letter of acceptance for my play in that stupid local contest. (*Pause.*)

JAKE: Really?

CLARA: Really! (*Shows the letter to JAKE.*)

JAKE: (*Reads.*) "I have the pleasure of informing you that your play entitled 'From Bondage to Freedom' has been accepted for production in the upcoming season. Thank you for your interest in the performing arts."

CLARA: HA! Take that! And this! (*Shows JAKE a ticket.*)

JAKE: Now what? (*Reads the ticket.*) Buenos Aires?

CLARA: (*Grabs back the tickets.*) Yes, a one-way ticket to Buenos Aires.

JAKE: You don't even speak Spanish.

CLARA: No, I don't, but Frankie does.

JAKE: Frankie who? (*Pauses. Scrutinizes CLARA.*) Not Frank Levin the salesman from Perfect Self-Publishing House?

CLARA: (*Triumphant.*) *Por supuesto, mi amigo! El mismo*, the very same. And I'm learning Spanish, too, and learning how to dance the tango and I'm enrolled in an expatriate English writer's club in Argentina that Frankie told me about, "*Las Gringas con Plumas.*" *Adios,* loser! (*Waves goodbye to JAKE as she strides past.*) It's been nice knowing you . . .sometimes.

JAKE: I guess you don't love me anymore?

CLARA: Love! I think I really do love you, Jake; I just can't live with you anymore.

JAKE: No final kiss?

CLARA: (*Shows her rear end.*) Kiss my ass, Kimosabee, I'm goin' out to sea! Tell me how the theater production goes and send me a review of my play. I'll be on the beach with Frankie working as his muse. (*Exits.*)

JAKE: (*Stands with papers in his hand.*) Conflict, passion and a dramatic arc with resolution of sorts. (*Makes a wide arch in the air. Pauses.*) Interesting dialogue. (*Pauses.*) This gives me some ideas for a new work. Yes, there is some real potential here. Maybe I can transform tragedy into triumph, a literary masterpiece from conjugal misery. (*Slumps down and shakes his head.*) Frank. Frank Levin. (*Looks heavenward.*) You've got to be kidding! (*Covers his face with his hands and sobs.*)

(*Lights go up on FRANK, who stands stage left, dressed in a tropical print shirt and dancing with CLARA to a sexy tango. FRANK and CLARA dance across the front of the stage and FRANK ends by twirling CLARA under his arm. Lights dim to dark. JAKE is alone on the sofa. Music may be "Hernando's Hideaway" or any other sensual tango, perhaps by Astor Piazzolla.*)

SCENE III: EATING CHICKEN (TEN MONTHS LATER)

(*JAKE sits in the same living room where he reads a book. He looks disheveled and aged. Knock at the door.*)

JAKE: Go away, whoever you are!

(*Knocking continues even louder.*)

JAKE: Okay! Okay. Come in, the door's open.

FRANK: (*Sticks his head through a crack in the door and looks in.*) Anyone home?

JAKE: (*Jumps up and crossed over to the door and pulls it open.*) YOU! (*Tries to slam the door shut on FRANK.*) Get out!

FRANK: (*Pushes the door open.*) Come on, now! We can be civil, can't we? (*Forces his way in.*)

JAKE: Get the hell out of here!

FRANK: I can explain everything. Really, I can.

JAKE: (*Grabs FRANK by the neck and begins to choke him.*) I bet you can, if I let you. Die, you philandering son-of-a-bitch!

FRANK: (*Struggles to free himself and stagger to the couch.*) I'm sorry! I'm really sorry about everything.

JAKE: (*Yells.*) Sorry about what, exactly? Lying to me? Stealing my wife? Betraying our friendship? (*Pauses.*) What exactly are you sorry about?

FRANK: (*Spins around and grabs JAKE's hand.*) I'm sorry for everything. Sorry about you, sorry about me, sorry about us, and sorry for Clara, too.

JAKE: (*Yanks his hand away.*) Save the crap! (*Points to the door.*) Now, get out! And I swear if you don't, I'll kill you.

FRANK: (*Takes a drink from the glass on the table.*) Bourbon? (*Drinks again.*) Yes, and a stiff one. You shouldn't drink alone, Jakie, that's how alcoholics get started. (*Finishes off the glass.*)

JAKE: (*Grabs FRANK by the collar and begins to drag him to the door.*) That's enough! Drinking with you would be worse than drinking alone. (*Pulls FRANK toward the door.*)

FRANK: (*Resists.*) Hold on! Don't you want to know why I'm here?

JAKE: No!

FRANK: I brought you a souvenir from Buenos Aires.

JAKE: (*Stops.*) My wife, I hope.

FRANK: Can we talk?

JAKE: (*Releases FRANK. Looks at his watch.*) Ten minutes! Ten minutes and not a second more!

FRANK: (*Brushes himself off. Reaches into his coat pocket and pulls out a book.*) Here! A gift.

JAKE: (*Looks at the book.*) This is mine. This is my manuscript.

FRANK: Yes, Jake. It's your book. Now look at the forward, written by Clara, the editor.

JAKE: (*Reads.*) "Dedicated to my ever-faithful husband, Jake Highlander, whose love of writing exceeds even his love for me." (*Sits down.*)

FRANK: Can I have another drink now?

JAKE: (*Stunned. Holds out the book.*) It's beautiful. Who did this?

FRANK: Well, it was Clara's idea and so I helped her a bit with the formatting and *voilà,* the finished volume from Perfect Self-Publishing Company. Your dreams become flesh, so to speak.

JAKE: (*Angrily.*) You're trying to buy me off with this book project. (*Throws it on the table.*) This is a cheap publicity stunt to pay for my wife, you philandering low-life asshole.

FRANK: No, not at all. We both thought you deserved it. (*Sighs*). Jakie, Jakie, Jakie. Do you know how to dance?

JAKE: (*Confused.*) Not exactly. Clara was pretty good at it, but I always had two left feet. In fact, she was a fine dancer.

FRANK: You're right! She's very good. (*Pulls JAKE off the couch.*) Come on, let me show you.

JAKE: (*Tries to pull away.*) No! I'm not in the mood.

FRANK: (*Insists. Pulls JAKE up.*) No, come on. Stand up. (*Puts his hand around JAKE in dance position.*) Now, this is a tango, a slow, sensual dance from Argentina. The American version is a bit simpler than the Argentine version, so I'll teach that. Now, it has five steps: slow, slow, quick, quick, slow. You start with the outside foot, your left. I'll be the woman, unless you want to be.

JAKE: No, thanks.

FRANK. That's right, start with the left forward. (*Explains the steps in a Tango rhythm.*) So, left, and right, and left, right, close. Now start again with the right. Slow, and slow, and quick, quick, slow. And again, left, right, left, right close and I turn you under my arm. (*Ends by turning JAKE in a dramatic finish.*) Great! You're a natural. Bravo!

JAKE: (*Pulls away.*) You betrayed me! I thought we were friends, literary soul brothers. I thought your really liked my work. I thought we had some spiritual connection around writing.

FRANK: And a physical one, too, perhaps? (*Gives JAKE a little caress.*)

JAKE: (*Pulls away.*) No!

FRANK: (*Picks up a glass and drinks.*) Too bad. (*Takes a swallow.*) You know, Jakie, sexuality is like a tree with a single trunk and many branches. (*Waves his hands around in the air.*)

JAKE: I'm part of that straight trunk.

FRANK: Many branches, remember? And every branch is as good as the next.

JAKE: Nope! Not my style.

FRANK: Clara's either, it appears.

JAKE: What is that supposed to mean?

FRANK: (*Walks around.*) Clara just couldn't adapt to the writer's group down there in Buenos Aires, *Las Gringas con Plumas.* They were mostly lesbian, with a smattering of bisexuals. I think she really tried very hard to fit in, but it just never worked out.

JAKE: So? You left her in Buenos Aires, you bastard.

FRANK: Oh no! But it was a pity because she was doing so well with her Spanish. Nothing like total immersion for learning a language and she's really very clever, too.

JAKE: So?

FRANK: Well, Jakie, that's my other souvenir! (*Points to the door. Yells.*) Clara, you can come in now!

CLARA: (*Enters wearing an elegant flowing black gown, which exudes sophistication. A colorful silk scarf wrapped loosely around her neck.*) Buenas dias, Jakie. I'm back!

JAKE: (*Rushes up to embrace CLARA.*) Clara, I'm so sorry! I'm so sorry! Forgive me for the way I've acted. (*Falls to his knees.*)

CLARA: (*Aloof.*) Not so fast. I'm just passing through. (*Notices the book.*) Did you like your book?

JAKE: (*Picks up the book.*) Oh yes! It's swell. (*Opens it and presents the book to CLARA.*) Please, sign if for me.

CLARA: (*Signs the book, hands it to JAKE and turns to FRANK.*) Any sales on Jake's book yet?

FRANK: Not a one, but a good-looking product, if I do say so myself.

CLARA: And a Pulitzer Prize, perhaps?

FRANK: (*Shakes his head.*) Nope, not yet.

JAKE: Stop it! Stop torturing me! If you've come her to make me miserable, you can both leave now.

CLARA: We're on our way to a book signing in New York. My book, of course. All the literati will be there. It should be a lot of fun.

FRANK: This signing will signal Clara's entry into the intellectual and artistic elite.

JAKE: (*To CLARA.*) I'm so proud of you.

CLARA: (*Skeptically.*) Really?

JAKE: Really! (*Pauses and looks from CLARA to JAKE.*) And you're not a couple?

CLARA: (*Looks at FRANK.*) Not except for dancing. Frank's my agent.

JAKE: Can I come to New York for the signing?

FRANK and CLARA: No!

CLARA: (*Pauses. Studies JAKE.*) Well, if you stay in a separate hotel and don't tell anyone I'm your wife, you can come.

FRANK: I guess you're right. He really can't do any harm, not at this point in your career. Who cares if he tags along? It might even by amusing.

CLARA: (*To FRANK.*) Someone who said I was like eating chicken everyday can certainly do me some harm.

FRANK: No one's going to listen to him, trust me.

JAKE: (*Rushes to CLARA.*) I've eaten chicken every day since you left: Chicken Kiev, chicken Provençal, chicken curry, Southern fried chicken, chicken nuggets, teriyaki chicken and chicken soup! Every day I ate chicken and dreamed of you.

FRANK and CLARA: Ugh!

JAKE: No! I really enjoyed it. I love chicken and I love you!

CLARA: And you're not bored?

JAKE: No, no! I've learned to enjoy the diversity, the beauty, and the creativity of chicken. I've learned to appreciate you, Clara, and I'm not going to make the same mistake twice. Come back home! Stay with me! I promise I've changed.

CLARA: So have I!

FRANK: So have I!

CLARA: But I'm not ready to come back and live with you.

FRANK: Me, either.

JAKE and CLARA: You weren't invited!

FRANK: What! (*To CLARA.*) I've taken you from obscurity and propelled you into national prominence. You were an unknown, miserable housewife and now you're a recognized author. Do you think that happened by chance? Do you really think you would have achieved celebrity in Jake's pitiful shadow?

CLARA: (*Looks from FRANK to JAKE and back again.*) Frank, you're a self-serving shit!

FRANK: (*Stomps toward the door.*) Clara, that's it! I'm calling McMillan and Doubleday and Penguin and telling them all I've been mistaken about you. You are not the next female Hemingway and they should forget you ever existed. (*Pauses.*) I'm an agent, not a charity. (*Looks from CLARA to JAKE.*) And certainly not a marriage counselor! You deserve one another. That's all I can say. And neither of your deserve me!

CLARA: Do you remember my gypsy grandmother's hunting knife?

FRANK: That was a lifetime ago.

CLARA: (*Pulls a knife off the table.*) This one, you pompous, parasitic sleaze.

FRANK: (*Backs away.*) Don't do anything rash! You're throwing away fame and fortune for this self-deluded hack!

CLARA: Shut up!

FRANK: You're the one who said that, not me. You called him a "self-deluded hack," remember?

CLARA: And I can say something like that to someone I love. But you can't and I'm sorry I ever did. Jake has more kindness in his little finger than you have in your whole wicked body.

FRANK: Your choice, bitch!

CLARA: (*Throws the knife at FRANK. Misses. Lunges on the ground to pick it up.*) Next time's the charm.

FRANK: (*Rushes to the door.*) You're both crazy! *Folie à deux,* no doubt about it. You deserve one another. (*Exits and slams the door shut.*)

JAKE: (*To CLARA.*) Folly a deh? What's that mean?

CLARA: (*Turns back to JAKE.*) Two people who share a mutual mental illness. Sort of a pair of crazies. (*Gestures to JAKE.*) Come over here.

JAKE: (*Walks toward CLARA warily.*) Forgiven?

CLARA: (*Hugs JAKE.*) Forgiven, but not forgotten. (*Kisses JAKE.*) Let's go to New York together. Get your things. We've got a book signing to attend.

JAKE: My book, too?

CLARA: (*Shrugs.*) Oh, why not?

JAKE: How about some lunch before leaving?

CLARA: What do you have? Or should I bother asking?

JAKE: Chicken, of course, but I can send out for sushi?

CLARA: I'd love some chicken. It's great to be back home.

(*JAKE and CLARA laugh as they embrace one another. JAKE leads CLARA offstage. Lights dim to dark. Tango melody plays.*)

THE END

DANIEL IN THE LION'S DEN

MEDIA MADNESS

CUTTING OFF JOHN

RELEVANCE

GREEN-TINGED

CANCER AND CHARITIES

GETTING A PENILE IMPLANT

MEDIA MADNESS

CAST OF CHARACTERS

KATHY: Thirty something young woman, possible overweight and poorly dressed. Inappropriate make-up, too pronounced and in poor taste.

DANIEL: Distinguished older gentleman, dressed in a tie and jacket. Correct speech.

SETTING

Kathy's office. There is a large, ostentatious desk with lots of important looking documents and computers.

KATHY: You can't do something like that!

DANIEL: Why not?

KATHY: Because this event could be considered controversial. This could reflect badly on the Department of Mental Health? Who approved this project?

DANIEL: No one. This is the fourth year we've sponsored this event.

KATHY: Well, who approved it last year or the year before? Or ever, for that matter?

DANIEL: This has taken place for four years and has been a huge success. It reflects a positive image on the Department and shows concern for the citizens of our region.

KATHY: I don't care! Nothing should come out of your mouth about anything without my approval! (*Shakes her finger in the air at DANIEL.*) Do you understand!

DANIEL: This event is in the best interest of the community. It reflects our concern for the poor and medically underserved and it perceived that way by a grateful community. What can be wrong with that?

KATHY: (*Yelling.*) You don't get it, do you? You are not autonomous! It doesn't matter whether you care about anyone or not! You have one right and one obligation and that is to shut your mouth and do your job. And when we ask you to say something, then you can open your mouth. And the words that come out had better be my words or my boss's words, pre-authorized by me!

DANIEL: Are you so frightened? (*Pauses.*) Are you so scared of losing your job that you need to squelch any initiative from the field, even positive ones? Who are you anyway?

KATHY: (*Yelling.*) I am the Director of the Bureau of Public Relations of the Department. I answer to my boss and his boss, who happens to be yours, too. You have no civil service protection. You can be fired by a phone call and I swear I can help arrange for one if you give me any more crap.

DANIEL: We try and help people; at least that's what we're supposed to do.

KATHY: And so do I. And that help starts with me and my interests and my job that I want to keep it as long as I can.

DANIEL: Like you five predecessors in as many years?

KATHY: Yes, but longer than them, a lot longer. I'm not going to let some old fart upstart from Hicksville like you jeopardize my livelihood or my career because he cares about the people in his region and spouts misplaced lofty principles. (*Yells.*) Do you understand me?

DANIEL: Perfectly. You are scared to death and I am too old for that.

KATHY: No, you're not too old, you pompous, sanctimonious old has-been! You will know fear and I'll make sure of it. I'll have you so wound up you won't know your head from your rear end. And I'll have the pleasure of seeing your ass out on the street while mine is still warm in my comfy chair in this government office.

DANIEL: Are you so sure?

KATHY: As sure as you are arrogant!

DANIEL: How old are you?

KATHY: That's none of your business.

DANIEL: And what exactly is your degree?

KATHY: None of your business?

DANIEL: And how many languages do you speak?

KATHY: Who the shit cares?

DANIEL: Do you think it's appropriate for a thirty something year old with a journalism degree and a few years of experience to browbeat a regional director with three professional degrees, 30 years of experience, who speaks three languages and actually cares about the people and his job performance?

KATHY: Yes, I can and should browbeat you. And no, I don't give a crap about your age, experience, credentials or linguistic pretentions. I have a job to do and if you don't start obeying the rules, you'll be history. (*Pauses.*) *Comprendo*? Do you understand?

DANIEL: Perfectly. (*Pauses.*) Are you happy in this job?

KATHY: (*Settles back.*) Perfectly.

DANIEL: Really? You seem pretty stressed out to me.

KATHY: Don't give me any of your two-bit psychological counseling. Save it for your future clients, if you can get any?

DANIEL: You know that the event we've been sponsoring has been well received not only by the community, but also by my superiors?

KATHY: And mine?

DANIEL: Have you bothered asking?

KATHY: No.

DANIEL: Perhaps you should?

KATHY: Perhaps you should get out of my office now!

DANIEL: I'm serious. Call my boss. He'll either support me or throw me under the bus. It shouldn't be too hard to tell the difference.

KATHY: (*Thinks.*) Okay. If you promise you'll get out of my sight after that.

DANIEL: I promise.

KATHY: (*Calls.*) Hello. This is Kathy in Public Relations. I have Daniel here from Northeast Region Mental Health. We're discussing the fact that he did not follow appropriate channels for this upcoming event. Did you know about this? (*Listens.*) Yes, he said it has gone on already for four years but . . . . (*Listens.*) No, he did not say you had authorized it in the past, just that you knew about. (*Listens.*) We can't have any old crazy thing coming out from people in the field without my knowledge.

It would be chaos, and huge risk of confusion and anarchy. (*Listens.*) Yes, it is a question of control. (*Listens.*) I cannot distinguish between good initiatives that come out of rogue elements of the department and bad ones. That's the whole point. (*Listens.*) Yes, I know this is a highly anticipated and appreciated event in the community. (*Listens.*) Yes, I know it reflects positively on the Department. (*Listens.*) Yes, I am interested in the health and welfare of the citizens of our great state. (*Listens.*) Of course. Of course. Yes, I understand completely. (*Clicks off the cell phone.*)

DANIEL: And?

KATHY: Your boss wanted me to ask you how Public Relations could help make this event even a greater success. (*Pauses.*) So, what can I do for you?

DANIEL: Thanks. I think we've got it covered by ourselves. (*Pauses.*) I would appreciate it if you do not treat me like a disobedient child.

KATHY: (*Nods half heartedly.*) I can try.

DANIEL: I know you are under terrible pressure. I know you've been tasked with controlling every aspect of communications in the Department. I also know it's impossible. I want to work with you. I want you as a partner trying to strike a balance between promoting innovations and creativity and assuring some doctrinal uniformity. (*Pauses.*) I wouldn't mind knowing you better, but right now, my only goal has been to minimize contact between us because all of our interactions have been painful. How exactly can we work together in the best interest of the people of this poor, unhealthy state? That's what I'd like to achieve.

KATHY: (*Grimly.*) You won this time, but I'm young and you're old. I may look frail and weak, but don't be misled. Your star will set while mine is rising. (*Pauses.*) Go ahead, hold your meeting! Get the adulation of the community or even our leadership, but watch your back and when you slip up, remember, I'll be there to push you under the bus and enjoy doing it.

DANIEL: I'm sorry you feel that way. (*Hands KATHY a paper.*) Here's an invitation to the event. I'm told we're going to have a capacity crowd.

KATHY: (*Throws the invitation on her desk.*) Get out of here and remember, you slip, I push! This is a rough and tumble place and I want to leave when I'm good and ready and not a day before.

DANIEL: I understand. Good luck. (*Extends his hand to KATHY.*)

KATHY: (*Refuses to take DANIEL's hand.*) Don't be ridiculous!

(*DANIEL turns to leave, but turns back when KATHY continues to speak.*)

KATHY: And if you think the community will rise up and save you when you get canned, think again. There will be a few phone calls, perhaps a kind letter to the editor, maybe even a going away party with a cake. And then you'll be gone and this great bureaucracy will just grind forward without you or me for that matter. Now, just get out! I can't stand the sight of you or the sound of your voice. Get out! NOW!

(*DANIEL turns and exits. KATHY picks up the invitation and tears it into pieces. Lights dim to dark.*)

THE END

CUTTING OFF JOHN

CAST OF CHARACTERS

PETER: CEO of the company, father of Charles (and John)

CHARLES: Son of Peter. Younger man, probably in his late thirties

DANIEL: Partner in the firm

SETTING

Peter's office. Peter is sitting in a desk with lots of papers on it. There are a couple of chairs.

CHARLES: What exactly did you do with John's insurance?

PETER: You heard, it's been cancelled.

CHARLES: You can't do that! He's still sick as a dog and might be in the hospital for weeks or months, if he survives at all.

PETER: Yes, that's the problem. He may be in the hospital for weeks or months, eating up our company's insurance fund. First, I fired him for job abandonment and then I cancelled his health insurance. Painful, but perfectly legal and totally unavoidable.

CHARLES: You nasty bastard. You fire him while he's fighting for his life. What kind of a monstrous, inhuman thing is that?

PETER: It's not monstrous. Our company is self-insured as far as health insurance is concerned and John's illness has almost drained that account. If he survives, and continues to use up the money at this rate, we will have nothing left for the rest of the employees. Nothing!

CHARLES: So what? John is your son, for God's sake, your own flesh and blood.

PETER: He will have to apply for Medicaid. He will surely qualify and that way it will be the government's problem, not ours. I'm sure the hospital will figure out some way to accelerate his application so they can get paid something, anyway.

CHARLES: You are a piece of work!

PETER: You don't think this makes me sick, too? Seeing my own son suffer and perhaps die in front of my eyes. It's tearing my heart out and your mother's, too. (*Pauses.*) But there are over 100 other employees to consider, including your wife and your children. Who will pay your daughter's medical bills if there's nothing left in our insurance fund? Have you thought about that?

CHARLES: Leave my wife and children out of this!

PETER: Why? They are my grandchildren and your wife is my daughter-in-law. I love them, too. And who will pay for your daughter's complicated orthopedic surgeries in the future. Or those expensive medications she takes when there's no money left in our fund? What then? Are you going to pay of your pocket? Are you going to deplete your savings account, your children's college funds? Your retirement? A second mortgage, perhaps?

CHARLES: (*Pauses.*) Of course I would! I would empty every account if I had to. Any decent parent would do anything for his family, anything!

PETER: Even when that compromises the care of everyone else?

CHARLES: Yes!

PETER: Well, I don't have that luxury. John gets fired. He has used up every day of his Federal Medical Leave Act time and legally he could be fired. When that happened, his health insurance went, too. Unless, of course, he could pay COBRA and we both know there's nothing left in any of his accounts to pay for that.

(*Knock on the door. DANIEL enters.*)

DANIEL: Hello Peter. Hello Charles. Can I come in? (*Looks around.*) Am I interrupting anything?

PETER: No!

CHARLES: Yes!

PETER: We're talking about John. You know I fired him and his health insurance has been cancelled.

DANIEL: I had heard that, but I just wanted to make sure it was true.

CHARLES: (*To DANIEL.*) So you agree with this bullshit? As a partner, you can voice your opinion, even if I may not agree with you most of the time.

DANIEL: No, I don't agree. This company is supposed to project an image of good in the community and I don't think firing employees who are sick projects a very loving image, especially your own son.

CHARLES: Amen.

PETER: (*To DANIEL.*) You asshole. You benefit from this awful tragedy to take some cheap shots at me. You're a pompous, self-righteous prick and you ought to be ashamed of yourself.

DANIEL: Me! Ashamed! I don't have to be ashamed of anything. I told you that being self-insured was a risk. I told you that trying to save money on insurance sounded tempting, but only if our luck didn't run out. And now the fund is getting depleted and you have to fire your own son to get him off the insurance. I don't think I have to take any cheap shots. In fact, I would support you if you decided to keep paying. It's the morally correct thing to do.

PETER: We can't. Do you understand? We can't. There's no money left. There's less than $100,000 in the insurance account and that has to pay expenses for everyone, not just my son. We spend more than that in three months, which is fine when there were a couple of million or more in the health insurance account. But now?

DANIEL: Take it out of the company charity fund.

PETER: What charity fund?

DANIEL: Ah yes, the charity fund that you said was too expensive for us. The one you didn't want to create because charity was an individual responsibility not a group one. (*Pauses.*) Well, I'm here to say that I will help make the sacrifices to sustain the insurance account and keep your son on the payroll and on his insurance and I for one am willing to pay. He will survive and he will get better.

CHARLES: No one knows that.

DANIEL: I just have a feeling.

CHARLES: A feeling? You have a feeling?

DANIEL: Yes, I have a feeling and (*to PETER*) you should, too. Is there no loving paternal fiber in that stony heart of yours?

PETER: You shit! Why don't you shut up and go away? You have always been the source of everything rotten in this company. All the conflicts, all the arguments, everything upsetting, somehow you've been at the heart of it, while we're speaking about hearts.

DANIEL: (*To CHARLES.*) Do agree with your father? Am I the source of all the troubles and conflicts in this company?

CHARLES: (*Looks back and forth from DANIEL to PETER. Hesitates.*) You can't expect me to choose between a colleague and my own father, can you?

PETER: (*To Charles.*) Go ahead! You just told me I was wrong about John. You just told me I lacked any fatherly love for my own son. Choose this stranger over your own flesh and blood. Why not? Add insult to injury.

CHARLES: (*To DANIEL.*) I don't think this it the right time to talk about this. You do have a real knack for stirring up trouble, even when it doesn't exist. Why don't you leave?

DANIEL: Leave the room, or leave the company?

CHARLES: Both! You're upsetting my dad and he's already having a rough time of it. Show some compassion, for heaven's sake.

DANIEL: Heaven? Now you are going to evoke the heavens? That's touching. Your brother is fighting for his life. You father insults me, even though I want to help save your brother. And you want me to show compassion when I've already agreed to help shoulder the financial burden of your brother's illness. (*Looks between CHARLES and PETER.*) Well I guess the apple doesn't fall far from the tree, does it.

CHARLES and PETER: Get out!

DANIEL: I'll leave. And I hope to God you find some compassion somewhere. Perhaps John will get some from heaven. Fatherly love doesn't seem to extend beyond those present. (*Pauses. To CHARLES.*) Such a demonstration of filial gratitude, at least that's admirable I suppose. (*Walks out.*)

CHARLES: He's right. You can't treat John like you're doing and expect anyone to trust you, especially your employees. Each one will think they are the next to go. Who can have any confidence in you after this?

PETER: It doesn't matter whether they have confidence or not. Fiduciary responsibility trumps feelings.

CHARLES: (*Approaches PETER.*) Even paternal love?

PETER: (*Takes CHARLES in his arms.*) Even paternal love. (*Kisses CHARLES on the cheek.*)

CHARLES: (*Pulls away.*) I don't want your Judas kiss. I don't like Daniel, but at least I can appreciate his candor. What I can't appreciate is your hypocrisy. Don't tell me you're doing this for the employees. You're doing this for yourself so you don't have to empty your 401K. (*Shakes his head.*) You're a piece of work, even if you are my dad. (*Pauses.*) I think I need to be going, too. (*Walks toward the door.*)

PETER: We'll see you Sunday for dinner, won't we?

CHARLES: No!

PETER: Your mother needs you. She needs to prove to herself and to me that she still loves all of her children, the sick ones and the well ones. She needs to be the loving mother and grandmother.

CHARLES: At least to the ones with insurance. Is that it?

PETER: Don't insult your mother!

CHARLES: Does she agree with you about firing John and dumping him onto Medicaid, if he can get it?

PETER: She understands.

CHARLES: Well, I don't. And I hope my wife sends me to hell if I ever make a similar decision, so help me God!

PETER: You're upset. Take the day off. Cool off and come back tomorrow after a good night's sleep.

CHARLES: Good night's sleep! You've got to be kidding. I'm on call tonight. I won't get three hours of sleep, if that.

PETER: Can I take call for you tonight? Would that help?

CHARLES: I can't ask that degree of sacrifice from you, can I?

PETER: Of course you can. I'll do anything for you. You're my son, my flesh and blood; I can't lose you, too. Some day this desk will be yours and you will be making the decisions, even the tough ones.

CHARLES: How could I ever make the company decisions? You'll die holding the company books in your cold fingers. It's all about the money and the power. Keep your desk and your decisions and your power.

PETER: Suit yourself.

CHARLES: Maybe Daniel was right; he said the oak and the cypress don't grow in each other's shadow. (*Takes a deep breath.*) It's time for me look for some sunshine.

PETER: (*Laughing.*) Where, in Daniel's shadow, that pompous, self-absorbed asshole?

CHARLES: No, not in his shadow either. Maybe I need to become my own man in another town in another state.

PETER: And throw away everything I have done for you, everything I have created for you both. It's all waiting for you if you just show some patience.

CHARLES: Keep it! And give my share to John, if he survives. (*Walks away.*)

PETER: At least he might appreciate what I do for him!

CHARLES: (*Turns to look back. Laughs.*) You've got be to kidding. Yeah, tell that to his widow and his fatherless children if he doesn't make it. Or perhaps I will? I'm sure she'll be impressed in either case. (*Shakes his head.*) God have mercy on your twisted soul!

PETER: (*Watches him leave.*) You'll be back! You'll come back crawling on your hands and knees when you can't make it out there without my help! Then you'll thank me. You'll see! (*Sits down and looks at the papers. Takes his head in his hands and shakes it.*)

(*Lights dim to dark.*)

THE END

RELEVANCE

CAST OF CHARACTERS

DANIEL: Middle-aged man, well dressed, very conservatively. Partner.

JOHN: Middle-aged man, more casually dressed. CEO of the company.

MARIA: Middle-aged woman, casually dressed. John's wife.

SETTING

The stage contains only a desk and chairs. It can be more elaborate, but does not need much detail. It is John's office.

DANIEL: What do you mean, I'm no longer needed?

JOHN: Just what I said. You're services are no longer required. Your skill sets are no longer relevant to the organization.

DANIEL: You can't just eliminate me like that! I'm a partner, not an employee.

JOHN: We're not eliminating you. You're being offered the opportunity of leaving on your own, or being voted out by the partnership.

DANIEL: Voted out? Do you know for a fact you have the votes for that?

JOHN: Not exactly. But are you willing to find out? You just keep spouting your crazy ideas that no one is interested in or wants to hear.

DANIEL: Like giving money away?

JOHN: Exactly! We're not here to give money away.

DANIEL: Even if it makes you more in the long run? It's an investment in the stability and longevity of the firm.

JOHN: (*Angrily.*) Will you stop your insane driveling! When will you wake up? You live on some far off planet. You're a visionary, a prophet with no followers. You cost this firm money, you drive away clients and now you can go your own way or the rest of us can push you there. Which do you prefer?

DANIEL: I see. I see where this is going. (*Pauses.*) You think when I'm gone all the problems and conflicts will suddenly disappear?

JOHN: Yes, I do, and your soon-to-be-ex-partners all believe the same way. You're a troublemaker and you bring conflict that no one wants.

DANIEL: Conflict! You don't want conflict, but you'll have it, with or without me. You'll have conflict with regulatory agencies swarming all over you in no time! How do you think outside payers think you make all that money you salivate over? Honest labor? Or maybe a little inside racketeering, with a few kickbacks here and there? A little creative billing? A little of providing expensive services that clients don't need or really want? (*Pauses.*) How long do you think that it will take until this place is crawling with auditors?

JOHN: That will be our problem, not yours.

DANIEL: Yes, until they want to verify who benefitted from your so-called essential services and call in every former partner to testify.

JOHN: (*Calmly.*) We need to end your association with this group on a positive note. We don't want screaming or yelling or. . . .

DANIEL: Lawsuits?

JOHN: You don't stand a chance so don't bother. We've already checked.

DANIEL: No? But perhaps you don't want too much scrutiny or publicity? (*Pauses.*) Or for me to take my clients with me?

JOHN: Our clients! Not your clients.

DANIEL: Really? I slaved decades to build a faithful clientele. Without an exclusion clause, I can set up down the street in a month.

JOHN: You'd better not!

DANIEL: And what exactly will keep me from doing it?

JOHN: (*Calmly.*) Because you have too much integrity. You're not interested in screwing people, even us. Besides, setting up your own business would be more trouble than I think you're willing to handle.

DAREN: How do you know that?

JOHN: Because you're spiritual and idealistic and burned out. And besides, you're the "conscience of the firm," isn't that right. Isn't that what the other partners call you?

DANIEL: Yes, and that makes you what?

JOHN: What does that make me, Daniel?

DANIEL: I think you know.

JOHN: No, I don't. WHAT DOES THAT MAKE ME?

DANIEL: (*Shakes his head.*) What's the point?

(*Phone rings. JOHN takes a cell phone or picks up a desk phone.*)

JOHN: Yes. (*Listens.*) This really isn't a good time. I'm in the middle of an important meeting. (*Listens.*) Yes, I know you don't care. (*Listens.*) Just stay out in the lobby a few minutes. (*Hangs up.*)

DANIEL: Bad time?

(*MARIA bursts into the room and confronts JOHN.*)

MARIA: You philandering son of a bitch! (*Turns to look at DANIEL.*)

DANIEL: Am I in the way?

MARIA: No! The more the merrier.

JOHN: Yes!

MARIA: (*To JOHN.*) I don't care if he does hear! Your whore from the office just called me up and said you were leaving me for her. Is that so?

JOHN: I never said that!

MARIA: Really? Well she said you did.

JOHN: She's lying.

MARIA: Like you!

JOHN: (*Glancing at DANIEL.*) Don't you think we ought to talk about this some other time? Daniel may not be interested.

DANIEL: Oh, I find it very interesting. As in private life, so in business, perhaps?

MARIA: (*To DANIEL.*) Oh, shut up, you busy body!

217

JOHN: I was just telling Daniel that his services were no longer required at the firm.

MARIA: Well, your services aren't required at home either, you prick! Go service your whore and leave me alone.

JOHN: Shut up!

MARIA: NO!

> (*JOHN moves toward MARIA with his hand raised. MARIA catches his hand in her left hand and gives him a slap with the right. JOHN steps back, holding his face with his hand.*)

DANIEL: (*To MARIA.*) You want me to help?

MARIA and JOHN: NO!

MARIA: (*Turns to DANIEL.*) You pompous, sanctimonious good-for-nothing meddler!

DANIEL: Hey! Don't get mad at me. I was just leaving.

MARIA and JOHN: Good!

MARIA: (*To DANIEL.*) I don't need anyone to tell me how bad my husband is. Just go back to where you came from, wherever that is, and leave us along. Take your foreign ideas and liberal notions. Maybe that's what's polluting my husband? Maybe your free love, charitable giving notions turned John's head, just like that little whore did.

JOHN: I won't give him that much credit. But his attitude is costing the clinic money.

DANIEL: You're both off your rockers. Free love and charity. They all called me the "conscience of the firm." Not the free love guru. (*Pauses.*) I've got the same wife and the same car and the same house I had 20 years ago. (*Pauses.*) Please go ahead and tear each other apart and I'll leave in peace.

MARIA and JOHN: Then go!

(*MARIA and JOHN point off-stage. DANIEL starts to leave.*)

DANIEL: Shouldn't it be the other way around? I thought the original sinners needed to go from the Garden of Eden, not the "conscience of the firm." (*Starts to walk off stage, but turns to look at MARIA and JOHN.*)

MARIA: (*Yells at DANIEL.*) Ah, you think you're God now, expulsing us sinners! You always did think you were superior to everyone. And I'm sure you think you still are, you shit!

JOHN: (*To MARIA.*) See! He made me crazy with all of his talk. He made me do it. He's the cause of all of our troubles. (*Takes MARIA in his arms.*) Things will go back to normal now. We'll get back to making money and not worrying about giving it away. We'll build that new house and get that condo at Aspen and take that Tuscan vacation you've always wanted. We'll make more money than ever and the whole family will prosper.

MARIA: And you'll leave that whore alone?

JOHN: Cross my heart and hope to die. (*Crosses his heart.*)

MARIA: (*Softens.*) If you don't, I'll make sure you will die.

DANIEL: How touching. (*Wipes a tear from his eyes.*)

MARIA and JOHN: Still here?

DANIEL: I'm leaving. (*To JOHN.*) This will be a good firm, but never a great one.

JOHN: I don't want greatness, I want money!

DANIEL: Seek first the Kingdom of Heaven and all things will be granted unto you.

MARIA: (*Screams.*) Get out, you hypocritical foreign piece of shit!

(*DANIEL leaves, shaking his head.*)

MARIA: Ouf! He's finally gone. (*Pauses.*) Do you think I was too over-the-top? All that whore business and screaming?

JOHN: (*Hugs her.*) You were perfect!

MARIA: And you really don't have a whore on the side, do you?

JOHN: (*Hugs her again.*) Of course not, I wouldn't dream of cheating on you. You know I believe in God, family and work, in that order. (*Looks at MARIA.*) You were really perfect. It was a great performance.

MARIA: You too, honey. (*MARIA kisses JOHN.*) Maybe we can go back and have some fun in that little break room in the back.

JOHN: Nah. It's not empty. We've stacked records and old equipment in there. It's very dirty. The lights are not working. It's just a mess. (*Takes MARIA by the arm.*)

MARIA: Really?

JOHN: Really. (*Leads MARIA stage right.*) I'll take you lunch at that new Italian place down on Lafayette Street. You know, the one with the gold letters.

(*Something falls in the back room, creating a loud clatter. MARIA and JOHN stop.*)

MARIA: What was that?

JOHN: (*Pulls MARIA in the opposite direction.*) Nothing. Something fell. It's a mess back there.

MARIA: Really? Something fell or someone fell?

JOHN: Don't be ridiculous. It's just a box or files.

MARIA: (*Pulls away from JOHN and goes to the back room door.*) Let me see for myself.

JOHN: Don't do it!

MARIA: (*Pulls open the door and looks inside. Opens her mouth. Slams the door shut and turns to JOHN.*) You miserable son-of-a-bitch! (*Rushes toward JOHN. She pounds JOHN while she swings her purse like a club.*) She was back there all the time! Just sitting there! You lying bastard! (*Continues to pound JOHN.*) I've scraped and lied and perjured myself for you and all the time your little whore really was back there.

JOHN: I can explain.

MARIA: I don't want your explanations. Daniel was right. He was right all along about you and me and that whore in the little room. This firm is a Godless, stinking pit. (*Pulls out her phone.*) I'm calling Daniel.

JOHN: What for?

MARIA: To apologize. To let him know that he is welcome to stay and clean up this moral morass.

JOHN: It won't make any difference. He's going to be voted out of the clinic whether I have a little piece on the side or not. (*Points to side room.*) She has nothing to do with management.

MARIA: Maybe, but it has everything to do with our life. (*Pauses. Talks on the phone.*) Daniel? Yes, this is Maria. I wanted to let you know. . . .(*stops.*) He hung up on me.

JOHN: Good! And I think you ought to get out of here as well. And if you want to get on your moral high horse, then do it, but kiss that new house and that beachfront condo and all the rest goodbye.

MARIA: I'm leaving. (*Walks to the door on the other side of the stage.*) Stay here and enjoy your whore. I'm done acting. I don't care about the consequences. You wanted to have your cake and eat it, too. So now you can choke yourself on it. (*Leaves the stage.*)

JOHN: (*Alone on stage. Sighs. Calls to the back room.*) You can come out now! I think she's gone for good. (*Yells.*) And how about trying out that new Italian place in town? I hear the lasagna's terrific.

(*Lights dim to dark.*)

THE END

GREEN-TINGED

CAST OF CHARACTERS

DR. DANIEL MASON: Middle-aged physician, dressed in a lab coat and tie.

WANDA COURTNEY: Older women, well dressed and somewhat abrasive speech pattern.

COLONEL VANDERLICK: Older man, casual attire, but an erect, military bearing. He has a Hitler like mustache.

NATALIE MASON: Daniel Mason's wife, an attractive, middle-aged woman with an elegant, but simple dress.

SETTING

Dr. Mason's office. There is a desk and laptop computer. There are papers stacked neatly and some awards or other objects. There is a chair in front of the desk and perhaps an oriental carpet to tie the room together visually. All of the characters, except Dr. Mason, have a distinctive green-tinted makeup.

WANDA: My back hurts so badly, I wake up at least three times a night. It's horrible. I think I'm losing my mind.

DANIEL: (*Leans closer to WANDA after looking up to see if there was anything wrong with the lighting.*) Yes, yes, I see.

WANDA: Are you even listening, Dr. Mason?

DANIEL: (*Draws back quickly.*) Of course I'm listening. You're having terrible back pains and it's keeping you from sleeping at night.

WANDA: (*Arches her thin tattooed eyebrows and pursed her thin, very red lips.*) I hope you're listening. For the money Medicare is paying you, I expect your full, undivided attention. (*Moves her head from side to side as talks.*)

DANIEL: (*Stands up and moves around to stand close the WANDA and scrutinizes the flesh around her ears.*) You seem to have a curious discoloration. It's like a sheen from the fluorescent light. I don't think I've ever seen the likes of it. It looks greenish.

WANDA: (*Ignores the observation.*) And I'll tell you another thing, I went to that Dr. Baxter, the rheumatologist, and he's a quack. He started me on these expensive medications full of side effects and didn't even bother telling me to come back for lab work. Are you listening, Dr. Mason?

DANIEL: Yes, yes.

WANDA: What on earth are you looking at me like that? You're think you'd seen a ghost, or a leper.

DANIEL: No, no. It's definitely not leprosy. I've seen that. It's something else.

WANDA: (*Looks at her flesh.*) There's nothing wrong. Can you concentrate on my problems with Dr. Baxter? I said he almost killed me with those immunobiologics or whatever you call them.

DANIEL: Yes, immunobiologicals. They're all the rage and very expensive.

WANDA: Do you think I ought to sue him?

DANIEL: Sue who?

WANDA: Dr. Baxter, the rheumatologist.

DANIEL: Sue for what?

WANDA: You really are distracted today. (*Pauses.*) For not asking for the right lab work and for giving me expensive injectable medications with lots of side effects and not even trying anything safer and cheaper. That's malpractice, isn't it?

DANIEL: I. . .well. . .it's complicated. (*Pauses and picks up the chart.*) Mrs. Courtney, I'd like to go ahead and order some lab work to check out your liver functions and blood count and some other things.

WANDA: To do Dr. Baxter's work for him and see if I'm dying from that medication he injected into me?

DANIEL: No, of course not, I just want to check something out. Not even related to those medications.

WANDA: What? What are you wanted to check out?

DANIEL: (*Hesitates.*) As I mentioned, I think your skin has a peculiar color.

WANDA: What color did you say?

DANIEL: Green.

WANDA: (*Laughs out loud.*) Okay. I thought that's what you said. (*Examines her own skin.*) Looks okay to me, but you're the doctor?

DANIEL: I might be wrong about your greenish tint and lab tests might be a useless expense, but if you have something real, something serious, I don't want to delay the diagnosis by not asking for lab work.

WANDA: (*Looks skeptical.*) Green, eh?

DANIEL: Greenish. (*Takes a piece of paper and hands it to her.*) Here are some lab orders. You need to stop by our lab on the way out. The results should be back in a few days and I'll be on the lookout. I'll give you a call if anything looks out of order.

WANDA: (*Takes the paper.*) Okay, you're the doctor. (*Looks at her arms and shakes her head.*) Green. (*Leaves the room.*)

DANIEL: (*Makes some notes and punches the intercom.*) Could you send in Mr. Vanderlick? Thanks. (*Rechecks the light and looks up at the ceiling.*) Odd, very odd.

COLONEL: (*Walks in a sits down in the chair with an air of authority. He, too, has a distinct greenish tinge on his face and hands.*) Hello, doctor.

DANIEL: (*Walks over and shakes the COLONEL's hand.*) Good afternoon, Colonel. How are you feeling today?

COLONEL: Fine, fine. Never better.

DANIEL: (*Returns to his seat at the desk. Flips through the chart or consults the laptop. Leans in to examine the COLONEL more closely.*) I'll be darned.

COLONEL: (*Returns the inquisitive stare.*) Are you okay, Dr. Mason?

DANIEL: Yes, yes of course. What about you? How do you really feel?

COLONEL: Fine, really. No problems.

DANIEL: What about your visit to the urologist? Dr. Hartman, I believe. How did that go?

COLONEL: (*Makes a sour face.*) That guy didn't even get my PSA.

DANIEL: Rules have changed. We are not recommending getting a Prostate Specific Antigen in older men anymore. Frankly, they are more likely to die from something besides prostate cancer than from the cancer itself even if they have it. In other words, most older men die with their prostate cancer but not from it. He should have explained the pros and cons of the testing at your age.

COLONEL: (*Slams his hand down on the desk.*) He didn't explain shit! That guy is so busy making money he can't even see straight. What if I turn out to have prostate cancer and he didn't even check? That would be a delay in diagnosis, wouldn't it? You can sue for that, can't you?

DANIEL: (*Draws back.*) Dr. Hartman is a very fine urologist. I've worked with him for years. He cares about his patients and their outcomes.

COLONEL: And what if I turn out to have prostate cancer? Can I sue him for that? Wouldn't he be depriving me of chance or something? You've seen the billboards, haven't you? What is my case worth?

DANIEL: (*Seems to ignore the comment. Goes to the COLONEL and moves his face from side to side.*) There's something odd about your skin color.

COLONEL: What's going on? Am I sick?

DANIEL: I don't know. I don't think so, but you have a greenish hue that doesn't look normal to me.

COLONEL: Green?

DANIEL: Yes. I may be mistaken, but I think you are a little green-tinged. I'd like to get some lab work to check it out. It's not a common coloration at all.

COLONEL: I don't feel sick.

DANIEL: You may not be, I just want to get some lab work to check it out.

COLONEL: (*Frowns.*) Do you own your own lab?

DANIEL: Yes, It's very convenient for patients.

COLONEL: (*Tilts his head to one side.*) Isn't that some sort of ethical violation? Self-referral or something like that?

DANIEL: I believe you're referring to the Stark Law. (*Makes some sort of notation in the chart.*) You are correct about that, but office labs are exempt because of patient convenience.

COLONEL: And do you own the hospital, too? Isn't that self-referral?

DANIEL: No, I don't own the hospital or the lab or the new surgery center. (*Places his stethoscope on COLONEL's chest over his clothes.*) Sounds good.

COLONEL: Hummph. How can you hear anything through three layers of clothes? You doctors are all the same. It's a show, an expensive one at that. And I may yet have prostate cancer, and maybe's it's turning me green. Dr. Hartman will hear from me and from my lawyer. You know, the one on the billboard. I'll get him. He always makes a killing, at least that's what they say in the paper.

DANIEL: Aren't you jumping ahead a bit here. We don't know what you have or what it means.

COLONEL: You doctors are all the same, just defending one another at the expense of the citizens. (*Pauses.*) I have every right to sue the whole lousy bunch of you. Men in white, men in black, you're all the enemies.

DANIEL: (*Hands the COLONEL a paper.*) Take this to the lab and lets start with that. I can't say for sure, but maybe there's some sort of epidemic.

COLONEL: Epidemic? Prostate cancer can't be catching. What are you going to do? (*Grabs the paper.*) I'll get this taken care of, but I hope if there's someone out there with the same problem, you'll start the process of containing this epidemic a little sooner. I could be dead before any doctor makes a diagnosis. It's disheartening. It's shameful. It's malpractice.

DANIEL: It's more complicated than that.

COLONEL: I need to get this taken care of as soon as possible. And be sure to call me with the results. None of this "No news is good news crap."

DANIEL: Of course.

(*COLONEL exits. DANIEL slumps to his chair. NATALIE comes in and sits in one of the chair. DANIEL looks up and sees NATALIE, who has a distinctly green hue. DANIEL gasps.*)

NATALIE: Well, aren't you even going to give me a welcome kiss? (*Notices his surprise.*) You'd think you'd seen a ghost. What on earth is the matter?

DANIEL: What's going on?

NATALIE: Why do you ask?

DANIEL: You don't look normal. You look. . .greenish. (*Pauses.*) There's something wrong and I suspect it has something to do with lawyers.

NATALIE: (*Looks shocked.*) How did you know?

DANIEL: Know what?

NATALIE: That I had seen a lawyer.

DANIEL: I knew it has something to do with lawyers. All day my patients have been talking about lawyers and suing and they all have this same greenish discoloration.

NATALIE: (*Interrupts him.*) I'm filing for a divorce.

DANIEL: (*Looks shocked.*) What are you talking about? We were planning on going to Bermuda on a second honeymoon? Divorce for what?

NATALIE: Irreconcilable differences.

DANIEL: What are you talking about? I love you. I need you. I've given you everything.

NATALIE: It's nothing personal. I just want to benefit from some time and attention before it's too late. I need someone who really sees me, who really sees who I am and what I need and want. You don't see me.

DANIEL: Yes I do, and you're green. Your face, your hands, your arms. You're green. You have some sort of illness, some virus.

NATALIE: (*Looks at her hands.*) No I'm not. You're delusional. You work too hard and you need a rest. You'll have plenty of time on your hands in the evenings. (*Stands.*) And I can go about my life.

DANIEL: It's another man, isn't it?

NATALIE: No, of course not.

DANIEL: It's that lawyer, Couillon, isn't it? He's been looking at you for years. (*Goes around the desk and grabs NATALIE.*) Tell me it's not true!

NATALIE: (*Pauses.*) It is true! It is Couillon, and the sooner he can get those papers are served, the happier I'll be. (*Pushes him off.*) Now leave me alone. I'm outta here! (*Glances back.*) Enjoy this hellhole as long as you can.

DANIEL: (*Returns to his desk and sits down.*) Green. They're all green. (*Takes a mirror or shiny object and looks at himself.*) I'll get the bitch. I'll hire that Whittier guy and make her rue the day she ever saw me. I don't care what it cost. She's a bitch and she's going to pay. (*Looks at himself in a hand mirror.*) I'm green. I'm green, too. It's unbelievable. I'm turning green, too. (*Gets his jacket.*) Maybe it's contagious. (*Looks bewildered.*) But everyone? Would everyone turn green at once? (*Pauses.*) I gotta get outta here. I can't stay and watch this happen. (*Pauses.*) I'll kill myself. Then she won't get the life insurance. (*Takes a vial out of a desk or cabinet. Drinks.*) Ahhhh. I don't have to turn green. I can't do it. Not and be like the rest of them. I'd rather die. (*Puts on his jacket.*) One door closes and another opens. Maybe this one just happens to be the door of a mausoleum. (*Exits. Lights dim to dark.*)

THE END

CANCER AND CHARITIES

CAST OF CHARACTERS

DANIEL MASON: Middle-aged public health physician. He is dressed in a shirt and tie, without a jacket. He wears and official nametag. He does not have a regional accent.

EVELYN PARKER: An older middle-aged, conservatively dressed woman. She has a pronounced Southern accent, but not overwhelming.

FRANCES BONTON: An African-American woman, who may be overweight. She speaks with a Southern, African-American speech pattern. She is dressed in a simple dress and has neither make-up nor jewelry.

JANE HIRONDELLE: Slightly younger woman. More casually dressed, but not sloppy. Speaks with a discreet Southern accent. Has a David Yurman bracelet. Evelyn Parker's niece.

SCENE I (THE CANCER REGISTRY)

SETTING

Dr. Daniel Mason's office. There is a desk and a couple of chairs. The desk has several stacks of papers. There need not be a lot of items.

EVELYN: (*Leafs through one of the binders.*) Dr. Mason, you can't present this data!

DANIEL: What do you mean?

EVELYN: I mean you can't present this cancer registry data to the public.

DANIEL: None of this is really confidential. It's public record already, so it's available to anyone for the asking. Why is that a problem?

EVELYN: Because it shows a statistical increase in cancer deaths in a five mile radius of our processing plant. What do you think revealing this data is going to do?

DANIEL: Inform the public.

EVELYN: Inform the public! You're a fool if you think that. (*Pauses.*) It will only inform and inflame every greedy plaintiff's attorney in a five hundred mile radius and notify him or her that it's open season on Parker Enterprises. That's what it will do. (*Pauses.*) My family has been part of this area for five generations. We have provided work for thousands of residents, black and white. Our Foundation does immense good for schools, churches, community groups and cultural organizations. Do you, Dr. Mason, want to put all that in jeopardy?

DANIEL: Discussing these findings doesn't necessarily mean you have to pay anything. You're just confronting the issue, not burying it.

EVELYN: Not pay! You've got to be kidding. Win or lose, we'll pay. (*Stands and leafs through the document.*) If some connection, however tenuous, is established between Parker Enterprises and these cancer deaths, we will end up paying out on a class action suit that might cost hundreds of thousands of dollars to defend. If we lose, our company may cease to exist. All those jobs will disappear and the Parker Foundation may have to be dissolved. Do you really want that for this community, Dr. Mason?

(*A knock at the door. FRANCES lets herself in and comes up to the desk.*)

FRANCES: Excuse me. I'm Mrs. Frances Bonton here to see Dr. Mason.

DANIEL: (*Rises and Shakes her hand.*) I'm Dr. Mason. (*Indicates a chair.*) Please, have a seat, Mrs. Bonton.

FRANCES: Thanks, but I prefer to stand. My back hurts so bad when I sit too much.

DANIEL: (*Sits down. Points to EVELYN.*) This is Mrs. Evelyn Parker.

EVELYN: (*Rises and shakes FRANCES' hand.*) Pleased to meet you.

FRANCES: (*Does not extend her hand, but nods. Turns back to DANIEL.*) The lady at the State Cancer Registry called and said you had a report for me.

DANIEL: (*Looks to EVELYN, who remains unmoving.*) Yes, we recently received the report. (*Takes it a shows it to FRANCIS.*)

FRANCES: Well? What does it show?

DANIEL: It's a highly technical document with a lot of specific medical language about probabilities and population rates.

FRANCES: So what does it really show?

DANIEL: (*Sighs.*) It shows an increase in cancer cases within a five-mile radius of Bayou Degelasse.

FRANCES: You mean our community?

DANIEL: Yes, your community.

FRANCES: Lord be praised! I knew it. My father and uncles and brother all worked in that Parker factory. They all died of cancer, every one of them.

DANIEL: There are many kinds of cancer.

FRANCES: Yes, I know. A few people here died of lung and a few more died of pancreatic cancer, and then there were a bunch of cases of lymphoma and leukemia. And there were many more, too. Lots of 'em! And those were just the deaths among my relatives. When you include the whole community and those that moved out, it's even more.

DANIEL: Having high rates of cancers is not proof of a cause and effect relationship.

FRANCES: What does that mean in plain English?

DANIEL: It means that the presence of the factory here doesn't necessarily mean that it caused any cancers. Smoking causes cancer and some other types of working conditions cause cancer, like working on the railroad and shipbuilding and being exposed to asbestos. Besides, I suppose no one forced your family members to work at this particular plant.

FRANCES: What else could they do? They didn't even have cars back then. They could at least walk to the plant here. Everyone walked to the plant back then.

DANIEL: I'm sure that there were safety requirements, even in the past.

FRANCES: Yeah! There were masks, but no one could wear them in that heat for mo' than a few minutes at a time. My brother used to come home a black as pitch. And somethin' the same color used to get spilled into Bayou Degelasse. It killed everythin', even the crawfish and the cypress trees.

EVELYN: (*Rises.*) I think I need to be going.

FRANCES: Aren't you Mrs. Parker from the factory owner's family?

EVELYN: Yes, I am. And we have always been concerned about the health and welfare of our workers.

FRANCES: We were grateful to have jobs, Mrs. Evelyn. Those are good jobs, good benefits, and even health insurance back then when most places didn't have it. But that plant was killin' people. And if you're dead, what's the good of a paycheck or health insurance?

EVELYN: Mrs. Bonton, as Dr. Mason here mentioned earlier, there is no evidence that there is any causal relationship between our plant and any cancers at all.

FRANCES: (*Points to the registry.*) Then what is that all about?

DANIEL: This is brand new mortality information; it hasn't even been released to the general public yet.

FRANCES: New! We've been tryin' to talk to you or someone in your family for years. Just talk to us. We wanted to be good citizens and good neighbors. We wanted to be workin' and healthy, if it was possible. (*Pauses.*) Why am I meetin' you now for the very first time. I never seen you at one funeral of one man, woman or child from our community in the last forty years. (*Pauses.*) My uncle was a shift worder for thirty years. (*Pauses.*) Thirty years workin' for Parker Enterprises and he lives one lousy year after his retirement and not one person from the administration came to see him off.

EVELYN: I'm sorry for your loss.

FRANCES: (*Pauses.*) Dozens of deaths. Hundreds of losses.

DANIEL: Not necessarily related to the work environment, Mrs. Bonton.

FRANCES: So who's goin' decide? Who's goin' decide what caused what? Is there somethin' else here in this place that makes people die? Somethin' in the air? Somethin' in the water?

DANIEL: People smoke here. People eat and drink too much. People here do things they shouldn't and die young. There are a hundred explanations for an increase in cancer deaths.

FRANCES: I just want one decent explanation. (*To EVELYN.*) Did your plant kill my relatives, my friends, and my neighbors? And if it did, what are you doin' do to make this place whole again? You owe this community a lot. We helped make your profits. We helped fund your charities. Now we want justice!

EVELYN: Justice or money?

FRANCES: Both!

EVELYN: (*Starts to leave.*) Then you will have to talk this over with our corporate lawyer. What more is there for me to say?

FRANCES: Just apologize! Start with an apology for fillin' the air and water with toxins. Look at Bayou Degelasse, dead trees and black water. Not even a live crawfish. It's horrible and my brother's lungs looked like that, too. He got dissected for some ungodly reason and we saw 'em, two black lungs like filthy sponges. (*Pauses.*) Just say you're sorry, woman to woman, mother to mother!

EVELYN: I'm sorry for your personal losses. I am sorry when an employee gets sick and dies. We care about our people and we care about the environment, whether anyone believes it our not. (*Looks at DANIEL.*) I must be leaving. And I count on your discretion, Doctor.

DANIEL: I can only present the facts, not assign culpability. You and your family have done magnificent things for this area and I, for one, appreciate it greatly.

EVELYN: Including your pet project, that theater group, Creative Creatures Productions. Perhaps an elimination of operating funds might be in order, to cover potential litigation costs. And, of course, I will be speaking with the governor, your boss, about the quality of his public health appointees. The Governor has always demonstrated a consistent support for business and is a personal friend of my brothers.

DANIEL: Mrs. Parker, you can certainly do that if you wish. It is a fact, beyond a shadow of a doubt, that three quarters of all toxic producing plants are located in communities of color. I'm not making that up. It's a known fact.

EVELYN: Who knows why? Maybe it's cheaper to live next to a plant and that attracts people with less financial means. Maybe the property values around a plant go down and only poor people can live there? I don't know why that happens and frankly, I don't care. You've got a big mouth, Doctor Mason, and I think your boss may have to shut it for you.

FRANCES: Are you theatenin' the doctor?

EVELYN: No, ma'am! I'm just stating the obvious.

DANIEL: (*To EVELYN.*) Any other comments?

EVELYN: No! Any further communications to either of you will be through our attorney. (*Leaves.*)

FRANCES: (*Sits down.*) I'm sorry to put you in this situation.

DANIEL: Don't worry. (*Flips through the report.*) This is only the beginning, not the end. We need to find out what happened to these people. (*Points to the registry.*) And then we need to make sure that needless deaths are prevented, regardless of the cause. The search for truth is what's important here and there are only winners in that pursuit, no losers.

FRANCES: Amen! (*Gestures toward heaven.*) And the truth shall set us free.

DANIEL: Yes, ma'am, perhaps even free from my current job.

FRANCES: You'll get another somewhere. A good doctor is always hard to find.

(*Lights dim to dark.*)

SCENE II: CHOOSING CHARITIES

SETTING

> There is a simple table and a couple of chairs. On the table there are three low boxes marked "To Be Considered," "Accepted," and "Rejected." There are stacks in the "To Be Considered" and "Accepted," but the "Rejected" box is empty.
>
> (*EVELYN and JANE are seated at the table where they are sorting through files.*)

EVELYN: (*Looks at one of the "To Be Considered" applications.*) This one is for a grant for repairs of the pipe organ at the Zion's Hope Baptist Church.

JANE: That's the black church down in the quarters, right?

EVELYN: Yes. The pastor's a well-known man, a bit of a social radical, but certainly nice enough.

JANE: How do you know so much about him?

EVEYLN: When you've been born, raised and lived in a town as long as I have, you know just about everything about just about everyone. (*Pauses.*) So this one's an "Accepted" for the Foundation.

JANE: Fine with me.

EVELYN: (*Takes another file.*) This one is for that theater group, "Creative Creatures Productions." (*Frowns.*) This one is not getting funded, not a dime. (*Throws the application into the "Rejected" box.*)

JANE: I thought we gave money to that group for the last few years already.

EVELYN: Yes, we did, but not this year.

JANE: Really? Why not? It thought it promoted local creative talent.

EVELYN: Don't you remember those vulgar plays from last year? We'd never attended before and then we got to be assaulted with a skit about a gay Klu Klux Klan member who finds out he's black and in love with his brother-in-law, the Klan Wizard.

JANE: I thought it was funny. I laughed through the whole thing and so did you, if I remember correctly.

EVELYN: Yes, there were some clever moments, but the whole idea was simply not consistent with our Foundation's principles.

JANE: Oh, come on, Evelyn. Aren't we supposed to be supporting creativity and innovation in the community?

EVELYN: Yes, but not plays about gays and abortion and premarital sex, for heaven's sake. There was that one about vaginal warts and I couldn't eat cauliflower for months without thinking about it. We can't be associated with filth.

JANE: Lighten up! Can't we make an exception? Does it always have to be about God, family values and patriotism? We can take a chance from time to time.

EVEYLN: No! Our family stands for those values and so does our Foundation. We have lived here for generations and own most of five counties, all the trees in the forests, and all the shale underneath the ground. We stand for the establishment and not disorder, chaos and vulgarity.

JANE: (*Pouts.*) I think we should support Creative Creatures Productions. There are some well-know local people involved and they deserve our support, too.

EVELYN: (*Snaps.*) Well know for liberalism, vulgarity and maybe even communism. (*Slams down the paper.*) No! Enough is enough! The arts are only valid when they support wholesome family values, the establishment, God or hopefully all three. Do you hear me, young lady?

JANE: Yes, Aunt Evie, but we have our own family issues, don't we? A little homosexuality in Uncle Casper, a bit of Klu Klux Klan in Great Uncle Peter, a bit of fiscal mismanagement with Auntie Carol, who ran away to France with that woman actress. Was that so nice, so wholesome and admirable? Is that just worth sweeping under the rug, or perhaps it's worth discussing, too.

EVELYN: Of course it's worth discussing, behind closed doors and among immediate family, not all of the stage for every Tom, Dick and Harry to see. And certainly not with the Foundation's name plastered all over the posters and handbills. That's unacceptable! That's a travesty.

JANE: Supporting creativity is never a travesty. How can we support all of these other God-fearing, conservative organizations and leave this one group out? I don't agree. Let's pull out a few from the "Accepted" box and take a look. (*Yanks some papers from the "Accepted" box.*) How about denying funds to the Children's Museum or the Women's Shelter. (*Yanks out some more.*) Or the Salvation Army? (*Yanks out another.*) Or the other community theater. They've put on seditious plays like "An Enemy of the People" and "Atonement" and "The Laramie Project" and "Doubt," for heaven's sake. And let's not forget that wholesome production of "Angels in America." What about that one? Should we deny them, too?

EVELYN: (*Yanks the papers away and puts them in the "Accepted" box.*) Yes, we have supported them and yes, some of the subjects were difficult subject matters. But they were plays by recognized national authors, not inspired local fools.

JANE: And we would be certainly not want to give our stamp of approved to local sedition, is that it? We can support out-of-town liberals, but we wouldn't want to foster homegrown literary terrorism? God forbid!

EVELYN: Let the Creative Creatures write whatever they want! Let the produce whatever they want! (*Pauses.*) But not with our good money and not with our good name attached.

JANE: I still don't agree. We all have skeletons in our closet, as you know only too well.

EVELYN: And let them remain there, safe and sound. And, quite frankly, I don't care if you agree or not! I am the senior member of the committee and I have the deciding vote. And I vote that Creative Creatures Productions should not be funded. No! No! Never again! It's amazing how we are punished for trying to help the community.

JANE: As they say, "No act of kindness goes unpunished." (*Pauses.*) And what happens when Creative Creatures decides to write a play about our industries polluting the environment and causing cancer in local underprivileged citizens. Is that what you want? (*Pauses.*) You want a play about fracking and destroying the pristine aquifer that provides the whole city with drinking water? What then, Aunt Evie?

EVELYN: How do you know about that?

JANE: About what?

EVELYN: The purported association between our Parker Industries and cases of cancer in the African-American community?

JANE: This is the first time I've heard about it? Is it true?

EVELYN: NO! It's just a ploy by greedy lawyers to extort some money. And some of the same people are involved with Creative Creatures Productions. So there just might be a play about it one day. Would you like to see that performed for everyone to see?

JANE: Well, it would bring the issue to the public.

EVELYN: Oh yes, indeed. And maybe a class action suit will destroy our company and the Foundation. Is that what you want? You want to be penniless and vilified. Is that what you want?

JANE: No, of course not. But it's just plays, not reality.

EVELYN: Perception is more important than reality and you need to get your priorities straight, young lady.

JANE: But a play? About environmental pollution and cancer? Sounds fascinating to me.

EVELYN: Let them try! We'll have an army of lawyers on them so fast for defamation that it will make their stupid creative heads spin.

JANE: So that's how we support free speech? (*Pauses.*) And foster local talent?

EVELYN: No, that's how we fight bankruptcy and social chaos. And that's how we will operate this Foundation, with an iron fist and a vengeful vigilance now and for the foreseeable future and as long as the Foundation exists and we can control it.

JANE: We?

EVELYN: Me! And if you don't enjoy working with me, you can leave now and I will find a more congenial selection committee member from our family. Heaven knows there's enough of them. Is that clear!

JANE: Perfectly. I quit! I'll take my chances with the truth. Enjoy your work and your solitude.

EVELYN: (*Turns her back.*) Go, with my blessing.

JANE: Your blessing! How pretentious can you get? I don't need that or your money. (*Pleads.*) I thought you loved me! I thought I was your favorite niece. At least that's what you said. I thought you said that the Lord leads us in paths of righteousness for his name's sake.

EVELYN: (*Keeps her back turned.*) Leave the Lord out of this. I do love you, more than you can imagine at your tender, idealistic age. But love has its limits, just like culture does. (*Turns to face JANE.*) Jane, we don't have to let Creative Creatures come between us. We have to stick together, as family, united against a very hostile world. Letting these fools come between us would be a real life tragedy.

JANE: They already have come between us, whether you want it or not! (*Points to the papers.*) Enjoy your counter-revolutionary activities. And remember what my high school English teacher told me, "You're not living unless you're making trouble." Remember him?

EVELYN: How could I ever forget him? I helped your parents get that rabble-rouser fired by the school board and I'd do it again in a heartbeat.

JANE: You can't save me from myself, and you can't save me or the community from the evil outside world. So don't bother trying! I accept you for who you are, warts, greed, Botox and all! And I feel sorry for you even if you are still my favorite aunt. (*Tries to embrace EVELYN.*)

EVELYN: (*Pushes JANE away.*) Don't bother feeling sorry for me.

JANE: Goodbye Aunt Evie. (*Exits.*)

EVELYN: I'll do what I have to do and you can do what you have to do to make it in this mixed-up world. (*Turns back to examine a new file. She picks up Creative Creatures from the "Rejected" box.*) "Creative Creatures Production." Damn them! Damn them to hell where they belong! (*Rips up the page and throws it into the rejected pile.*)

(*Lights dim to dark.*)

THE END

GETTING A PENILE IMPLANT

CAST OF CHARACTERS

DR. DANIEL MASON: Middle aged man, well dressed. No regional accent.

RICHARD SMITH: Older gentlemen. Well dressed, a more coarse speech pattern. Appears in pajamas in Scene II.

MARY-BELLE SMITH: Younger woman. She appears in pajamas in Scene II. Vulgar speech pattern and language.

SCENE I

SETTING

A doctors's office with a desk and a couple of chairs. There is a laptop and a lamp on the desk. There is a screen that hides an examination area.

(*DR. DANIEL MASON sits at his desks and is using a laptop computer instead of a written file. This is the electronic health record era. RICHARD walks in and DANIEL rises to greet him.*)

DANIEL: Nice to see you, Mr. Smith. How are you doing today?

RICHARD: Not worth a damn!

DANIEL: What's the problem?

RICHARD: I'm only 55 years old and I can't get it up anymore.

DANIEL: I guess you're talking about erectile dysfunction.

RICHARD: You're damn right I am. My wife, Mary-Belle, is 20 years younger. She's my third wife and I just can't satisfy her anymore. It's a problem because I catch her looking at the pool man, really just a kid, with that hungry look, you know?

DANIEL: I can imagine.

RICHARD: Who the hell knows what she does when I'm out of the house, much less out of town on business?

DANIEL: So what exactly can I do for you?

RICHARD: I want a prescription for that roll on testosterone stuff I see on the television. I want my "T" up so the rest of me will be up, too. I want the good old days when an all-nighter was a three bang affair and morning after chaser. My God, those were the days.

DANIEL: Let me take a look at you before we go any further. (*Indicates the privacy screen.*) Please step behind the screen and drop you shorts. I need to look at your testicles and do a prostate exam.

(*DANIEL and RICHARD step behind the screen.*)

DANIEL: Your testicles look like they are normal size. Turn your head to the side and cough.

RICHARD: (*Coughs.*)

DANIEL: Now this side. Cough again.

RICHARD: (*Coughs again.*)

DANIEL: Now bend over and spread your cheeks.

RICHARD: Ouch! Doc, take your watch off first, will you.

DANIEL: Your prostate's enlarged. You might have trouble urinating. Here's a Kleenex to wipe yourself off back there.

(*DANIEL and RICHARD come out from behind the screen and take their seats by the table. DANIEL types into the laptop.*)

RICHARD: I can't pee. I can't screw. I can't hear without my hearing aides. And I can't see without my glasses.

DANIEL: (*Looking at the laptop.*) Your PSA level is elevated, too. Not a lot, but certainly above normal. Didn't you have a prostate biopsy awhile back?

RICHARD: Damn yes! That hurt like hell. That urologist shoved some kinda huge tube up my ass and proceeded to take snippets out of my prostate. Click. Click. Click. I could hear this awful clickin' sound, followed by a jolt of pain. It was torture. All that and they didn't even find any cancer.

DANIEL: Mr. Smith.

RICHARD: Call me Dick, please. I can't stand this formality, especially from someone whose had his finger up my ass.

DANIEL: Dick. (*Pauses.*) I can't give you testosterone.

RICHARD: Why not?

DANIEL: Because your prostate's enlarged and your PSA is elevated. And, besides, I don't even know if your testosterone level is low.

RICHARD: Then get a blood test and find out. It's got to be low they way I'm performing.

DANIEL: It doesn't matter. Testosterone can worsen prostate enlargement and increase your risk for prostate cancer.

RICHARD: You're making this up.

DANIEL: No, I'm not.

RICHARD: I've seen it on television. You just smear that stuff on like deodorant and then pop a Viagra or a Cialis and you're good to go. I've seen it.

DANIEL: Those are actors. You can't take testosterone. It's dangerous for you.

RICHARD: Don't tell me this stuff.

DANIEL: What? The truth.

RICHARD: I don't want to be an impotent old fart with a hot new wife. She'll be outta my life in a heartbeat. I don't wanna lose her.

DANIEL: There are implants.

RICHARD: Fake dicks? I'm not into those party favors. Women don't like 'em anyway. They never feel right; at least that's what I've heard.

DANIEL: No, I mean a real penile implant. The urologist can put something into the shaft of your penis and there's a little pump in the scrotum, with a valve on it. You just pump it up.

RICHARD: Does it work?

DANIEL: Apparently it does. At least that's what another patient tells me.

RICHARD: Can I talk to him about it?

DANIEL: No, that's a HIPAA violation, a breach of confidence.

RICHARD: (*Thinks awhile.*) So you just pump it up?

DANIEL: Right.

RICHARD: And when you want it to go back down, what do you do?

DANIEL: There's a little valve in the scrotum. You just push it and down it comes.

RICHARD: (*Thinks.*) I dunno, Doc, sounds pretty unnatural, real mechanical-like. (*Pauses.*) I can hear it now, "Honey, wait a minute while I pump myself up." (*Pauses.*) Doesn't sound very organic. Can I get an implant and not tell my wife?

DANIEL: Your wife needs to know. You can't keep something like that secret. And maybe she'll get used to it and even like it. She'll ask you if she can pump it up for you.

RICHARD: Like using a heated dildo.

DANIEL: Sort of.

RICHARD: This is all too weird for me. Just give me a script for the "T" and I'll take my chances.

DANIEL: No.

RICHARD: (*Stands.*) You don't have a heart, doc. Life is full of dangers. It's all about taking risks.

DANIEL: Yes, and in your case, the risks clearly outweigh the benefits.

RICHARD: How do you know? You don't know what's really important to me. Maybe I just wanna die happy and not this miserable old wreck you see before you.

DANIEL: I can't prescribe it.

RICHARD: No, you won't prescribe it. There's a difference.

DANIEL: No, I won't.

RICHARD: And when I die from grief from not satisfyin' her, I hope my wife sues the hell outta you for murder.

DANIEL: That's ridiculous and you know it.

RICHARD: People can sue for anything.

DANIEL: Not because I did my job and refused to prescribe something that was dangerous and contraindicated in your particular case.

RICHARD: No, because you're deprivin' me of the chance to be happy.

DANIEL: And healthy? What about the healthy part?

RICHARD: What's health without happiness? (*Pauses.*) I like you, Doc. But you gotta lighten up.

DANIEL: I can't and I won't prescribe you testosterone.

RICHARD: (*Sits down again.*) Okay. I'll just have to go on-line or go to that doctor down on Fullerton Street that gives anything to anybody for a price.

DANIEL: (*Stands.*) Mr. Smith. Dick. I've enjoyed taking care of you, but I can see we are reaching an impasse here. I still have the liberty to suggest you go to any doctor of your choosing, even that quack on Fullerton.

RICHARD: Don't lie. You haven't enjoyed takin' care of me. You can't have. I'm a pain in the ass. But you're a good doctor, just not very accommodatin'. Can I have my medical records?

DANIEL: Sure. They're electronic. I can send them anytime to anyone if I have the appropriate signed permission from you. (*Hands RICHARD a form.*) Here's a consent form for a release of information.

RICHARD: (*Sighs.*) I'll let you know who needs to get it. If you don't hear from me, then maybe I changed my mind. Life's unpredictable, you know.

DANIEL: If we don't see each other again, good luck.

(*RICHARD and DANIEL shake hands. RICHARD exits and DANIEL sits back down and begins to type on the laptop. Lights dim to dark.*)

SCENE II

SETTING

RICHARD and MARY-BELLE, both dressed in pajamas, are lying in a bed with a sheet or blanket over them. RICHARD may be bare-chested. One or both may be smoking.

MARY-BELLE: Well, that was big flop.

RICHARD: I know. Can't we try again?

MARY-BELLE: Why bother? You're as flabby as a corn dog. Come to think of it, I've had some corn dogs that were harder.

RICHARD: Oh, come on, Mary-Belle. Maybe you could do a bit of a hand job. That usually works.

MARY-BELLE: In case you didn't notice, I already tried. You musta forgot already. Maybe your memory's goin', too.

RICHARD: Mary-Belle, please. Please don't make fun of me. That only makes things worse. It affects my self-confidence.

MARY-BELLE: Makes things worse? How can they be worse? You can't hear without your hearin' aides. You can't see without your glasses. You can't pee without standin' twenty minutes over the toilet. And then you have to get up five times at night to pee anyway. And you can't even get it up, even with that underarm "T" stuff you got from that charlatan down on Fullerton Street. What am I supposed to do to get some satisfaction? I got my needs, too, you know.

RICHARD: Yes, I know. (*Pauses.*) What if I put in a special pump?

MARY-BELLE: (*Laughs.*) A pump? What kinda pump?

RICHARD: A little pump in an implant in the penis. You just got to pump it up each time you want to have sex.

MARY-BELLE: Like a bicycle pump? What do I have to do, pump you up each time to get a hard on? (*Laughs out loud.*) That's crazy. You gotta be kiddin'. (*Laughs again.*)

RICHARD: Stop laughin'. It's for real. Dr. Mason told me about it.

MARY-BELLE: I thought you got mad and left him.

RICHARD: I did. But he's a nice guy and he knows what he's talking about. He'll take me back and get this pump thing arranged. (*Excitedly.*) There's a little pump in the scrotum that you pump up and when you're done having sex, you push a little valve and it comes down. Plop, like that. Clean, easy and efficient.

MARY-BELLE: And oh so romantic! You gotta be kiddin'.

RICHARD: No, I'm dead serious.

MARY-BELLE: Well, that's pretty serious. By the way, is your life insurance paid up if you're dead serious?

RICHARD: Don't change the subject. Dr. Mason thinks it would work fine. Besides, he doesn't want me usin' that "T" stuff anyway. He says it can cause my prostate to grow and maybe even give me prostate cancer.

MARY-BELLE: Really? Is your prostate growing?

RICHARD: I dunno. But I can't pee worth a damn and it's worse since I started that underarm "T" stuff.

MARY-BELLE: I tried it, too, you know.

RICHARD: What! Don't do that!

MARY-BELLE: I thought it might make me more horny. An a-phro-disiac, of sorts.

RICHARD: You don't need anything to make you hornier. Besides, that stuff will make you grow a mustache and that's a real turn off to men.

MARY-BELLE: Ugh!

RICHARD: So, what do you think? You want me to give it a try?

MARY-BELLE: Try what?

RICHARD: The pump. Get a penis implant.

MARY-BELLE: That's great. You'll have defibrillator in your heart and a boner implant in your dick. Yes, that'll be great. I'll be afraid to touch you anywhere.

RICHARD: Seriously. It'll help me. It'll help us. That's what the doc said.

MARY-BELLE: (*Thinks a little.*) Why not? I guess I can get into pumpin' you up. It beats wasted hand jobs. Those things were just wearin' me out, and givin' me carpal tunnel, beside. I was wankin' you so hard, I lost the feelin' in both hands.

RICHARD: You can be so vulgar.

MARY-BELLE: (*Caresses RICHARD's chest.*) Vulgar, eh? I know you love it, don't you. (*Kisses RICHARD. Moves lower.*) Maybe somethin' more direct than my hand will do the job. (*Puckers up and lifts up the sheet.*)

RICHARD: (*Pushes her away.*) Don't bother. It's dead.

MARY-BELLE: You used to be up with a touch of the hand. Now even a blowjob don't do the work. Go for the pump. (*Pauses.*) You know that young pool guy?

RICHARD: Yeah, Fred or Frosty or something like that.

MARY-BELLE: Frankie is his name. (*Pauses.*) He's twenty, maybe even a bit younger and very buff.

RICHARD: So?

MARY-BELLE: That kid gets a boner when I walk within ten feet of him.

RICHARD: How do you know?

MARY-BELLE: 'Cause I got my eyes and I can see real good, even without glasses.

RICHARD: I hope that's all you do.

MARY-BELLE: Sweetie pie, I'm not dumb. Why would I risk my sugar daddy for a Kit Kat bar? (*Pauses.*) Anyway, he's poor as dirt and comes from some huge family. I think he's gotta a couple of kids already, by a couple of different girls.

RICHARD: So?

MARY-BELLE: So, maybe he needs some money.

RICHARD: So?

MARY-BELLE: So, maybe he'd let them do a penis transplant if you pay him enough. They could graft his dick onto you and you can give him yours.

RICHARD: You're so dumb.

MARY-BELLE: Why? They transplant hearts and lungs and kidneys and stuff. I even seen that they transplanted hands and even faces. Why not a penis?

RICHARD: You're not kiddin' are you?

MARY-BELLE: No, I ain't kiddin'. It's worth a thought.

RICHARD: Well, I don't know if they do that sorta thing. And most of the time it's from dead people anyway.

MARY-BELLE: So?

RICHARD: Oh, God. Don't go there. You'd be in prison and I'd have a new dick that I couldn't use. And you would be savin' your bananas for your satisfaction.

MARY-BELLE: I guess that was a bad idea?

RICHARD: Yes.

(*RICHARD and MARY-BELLE sit on the bed in silence.*)

MARY-BELLE: So go ahead and do it! Get the dick implant and the pump. Let's just go ahead and do it.

RICHARD: I gotta get cleared for surgery. At my age, everythin' is a risk. It's a risk just to get up in the mornin'.

MARY-BELLE: Dr. Mason suggested it. He must think you're able to get the surgery.

RICHARD: (*Kisses MARY-BELLE.*) Thanks, honey, I worry about you and your needs. I gotta give you some satisfaction.

MARY-BELLE: You're my super-sized sugar daddy. And soon you'll be my inflatable sugar daddy. (*Claps her hands in glee. Begins to make pumping motions with her fingers.*)

RICHARD: What are doin'?

MARY-BELLE: Practicin'.

(RICHARD and MARY-BELLE laugh and fall into one another's arms. Lights dim to dark.)

SCENE III

SETTING

Back in the Daniel's office.

(MARY-BELLE enters. DANIEL is working with his laptop at the desk. MARY-BELLE is dressed in sexy black, something almost like a Halloween barmaid. MARY-BELLE carries some papers.)

DANIEL: *(Rises to greet MARY-BELLE.)* Mrs. Smith, this is unexpected. First, let me express my sincere condolences for the loss of your husband.

MARY-BELLE: Can it doc! He's not lost, he's dead. *(Puts some papers on the desk.)* These are for you.

DANIEL: *(Picks them up and examines them.)* It's a lawsuit.

MARY-BELLE: You bet your ass, Doc, it's a lawsuit!

DANIEL: *(Frowns.)* Usually someone from the sheriff's office delivers these.

MARY-BELLE: *(Calmly.)* I know. They told me that, but I insisted on doin' it myself. I'm not afraid of you or any of your pseudo-knowledge.

DANIEL: *(Reads the paper.)* Failure to exercise due caution. Failure to inform. Failure to perform appropriate testing. Loss of consortium. Mental pain and suffering.

MARY-BELLE: Yes, all that and more.

DANIEL: I'm truly sorry about your husband's death. He was not a good surgical candidate, even for a small surgery and I told him that.

MARY-BELLE: Small surgery! You call puttin' an implant in his penis and a pump in his scrotum under general anesthesia a "small surgery?" You really are a quack! (*Goes into her purse and pulls out a card. Throws the card on the desk.*) And here's your so-called sympathy card back.

DANIEL: (*Reads the card.*) "You murdered him!" That's what you wrote on it?

MARY-BELLE: Yes, you murdered my hubbie and you're goin' pay through the nose.

DANIEL: Mrs. Smith, we probably should not be communicating under these circumstances. But you need to know that I liked and respected your husband. He knew the risks, alternatives and benefits of the implant procedure and he chose to proceed. That is all documented in his chart, along with his signed consent form for the surgery. Your suit might prove a long, difficult and painful process for everyone with no positive outcome for anyone.

MARY-BELLE: No positive outcome, eh? And what about a million dollars for me and Frankie?

DANIEL: Frankie? Your son by a previous marriage?

MARY-BELLE: No, my pool man.

DANIEL: (*Looks heavenward.*) Right, of course.

MARY-BELLE: My lawyer says this case is a slam-dunk. You sent a guy with a bad heart and a defibrillator into a useless, high-risk surgery. That's malpractice.

DANIEL: Your husband did not think it was useless. I'm sorry he died. I'm sorry for your loss.

MARY-BELLE: (*Weeps and then screams.*) You ain't half sorry yet, but you will be! My lawyer says this case is worth a ton of money. He says he'll have that jury wrapped around his little finger and you'll be cleaned out, along with the hospital and that good-for-nothing surgeon, too. I'll get a fortune.

DANIEL: I'm sure your husband left you well provided for.

MARY-BELLE: (*Screams.*) He didn't pay his life insurance premium. He took the money for the surgery 'cause the damn health insurance company wouldn't pay for and e-lect-tive procedure.

DANIEL: I'm sorry to hear that.

MARY-BELLE: I gotta do this! I gotta sue you. I gotta get some money or I'll be an old used-up tart with nothin' to offer and no money to live off. (*Weeps.*) I barely got Old Dickie interested in me as it was and I had to work like a dog to keep him busy. (*Slumps in the chair.*) I gotta do this and I wanna do this.

DANIEL: (*Reaches over to comfort MARY-BELLE.*) Mrs. Smith.

MARY-BELLE: Mary-Belle, please.

DANIEL: Mary-Belle, this lawsuit is going to go on and on and on and cost a lot of money to the insurance company and to your lawyer.

MARY-BELLE: Yeah, that's what my lawyer said. He's sure they'll wanna settle for a fat lump sum so it don't go to court. (*Plays with a letter opener.*) This is real nice. Where did it come from, Arabia?

DANIEL: Indonesia.

MARY-BELLE: That's somewhere in South American, isn't it?

DANIEL: No, it's in Southeast Asia.

MARY-BELLE: (*Takes a handkerchief out of her purse and blows her nose.*) Doc, you gotta pay me. I don't even really hate you. But you got insurance and they have a lotta money.

DANIEL: (*Picks up the paper.*) This isn't the way. It's not right.

MARY-BELLE: It's the only way.

DANIEL: With no money down and 30% for the lawyer.

MARY-BELLE: (*Surprised.*) No, 50%, 'cause it's a complicated case. At least that's what he says. (*Opens her bag. Returns the handkerchief.*)

DANIEL: (*Glances into the bag. Notices a recording device.*) You're recording this conversation, aren't you?

MARY-BELLE: Yes, I am.

DANIEL: Your idea?

MARY-BELLE: Well, mine and my lawyer's.

DANIEL: I'm going to have to ask you to leave.

MARY-BELLE: I'll turn it off. (*Does something in her purse.*) There! It's turned off. (*Goes over to DANIEL. Hangs over the desk.*) I've always liked you. You're handsome and speak really good English. Maybe you want to have some fun?

DANIEL: I'm happily married.

MARY-BELLE: So? (*Plays with DANIEL's tie.*) I'm lots of fun and I can be very discreet.

DANIEL: (*Pulls away.*) Mrs. Smith. . . .

MARY-BELLE: Mary-Belle, please.

DANIEL: Mrs. Smith! Please leave my office now! If you do not go, I'm calling the police.

MARY-BELLE: Do it! Call the police! Call the newspaper! Call the television! I want everyone to know what a quack doctor you are! You're a killer! I want everyone to know. You killed my husband and I want to do the same to you. (*Pulls a revolver from her purse.*)

DANIEL: (*Draws back.*) Don't do anything you'll regret.

MARY-BELLE: I already regret just about everything in my life. I regret my badass childhood, my three crummy marriages, my alcohol and drug use. If I gotta be poor, at least I'll be poor in prison where I'll get free room and board and medical care.

DANIEL: Mrs. Smith, Mary-Belle. Think of what you're doing.

MARY-BELLE: I know what I'm doin'. I hate you! You're alive! You're rich! You're happy! And I'm goin' be poor and miserable if my lawyer doesn't do what he says.

DANIEL: (*Approaches MARY-BELLE.*) Please, give me the gun.

MARY-BELLE: Stay back or I'll blow your balls off. (*Points to DANIEL's crotch.*)

DANIEL: (*Continues to approach.*) Please give me the gun.

MARY-BELLE: All for a fake penis. (*Shakes her head.*) A fake penis and now he's dead and I'm dyin'.

DANIEL: (*Continues to approach. Tries to day the gun.*) Give it to me, please.

MARY-BELLE: Don't! Don't get near me!

DANIEL: You're suffering. This isn't going to help. You aren't making good decisions. Give yourself some time to grieve. Don't do anything before a year. You're depressed after your husband's loss. That's natural. You need time to reorganize your life, to weigh your options. You must give yourself some time.

MARY-BELLE: (*Screams.*) I don't have any time, Doc! I don't have any more options. I got breast cancer and it's spread all over my body. I'm really dyin' and I'm alone. I don't wanna die alone.

DANIEL: And Frankie? Your pool boy?

MARY-BELLE: He's already gone. He just wanted the money he thought I'd get. (*Looks back to DANIEL.*) I don't wanna die alone and I don't have to, either. I'm sorry for you and Dickie and me, but I ain't dyin' alone, Doc. (*Shoots the gun.*)

(*DANIEL falls to the ground. MARY-BELLE points the gun at her own head and shoots. Falls over DANIEL. Lights dim to dark.*)

THE END

HOOK, LINE AND SINKER

CAST OF CHARACTERS

DR. HAROLD CARDINAL: Older orthopedist. Somewhat pedantic. Obviously beyond his prime. Dressed in a starched lab coat, perhaps a bit wrinkled.

LAURA TATUM: Older woman. Not elegantly dressed, but clean and presentable. Speaks with a noticeable, but mild Southern rural accent.

JONATHAN DAVIS: Plaintiff's attorney. Dressed in a suit and tie. Formal and stiff in his attitude and speech.

DERRICK SHARP: Defense attorney. Dressed in a blazer and grey pants, with a shirt and tie. No regional accent.

SETTING

The setting varies with the scene. Scene I is a doctor's office, with minimal set elements. Scene II is a lawyers' office with minimal set elements. Scene III is a courtroom with only a raised platform with a chair as a "witness stand." Scene IV is a small meeting room with a couple of chairs.

SCENE I

(*DR. CARDINAL's Office. There is a desk and a couple of books. A stethoscope is casually draped around his neck. He is dressed in a starched lab coat. There is a chair for a guest. Minimal set elements required.*)

HAROLD: (*Slams down a phone or punches an I-phone to show it being turned off.*) How dare he? How dare he second-guess me? (*Pauses.*) And for what? (*Shakes his fist.*) Damn that little pipsqueak! (*Stands up and wanders around the stage.*) He'll rue the day he ever called me, by God!

He'll think twice before he calls and challenges my clinical judgment. And the day before the scheduled surgery no less! God damn him to hell!

(*Buzzer sounds.*)

HAROLD: (*Bangs down on a button.*) Okay, okay. Send her in. I'm ready.

LAURA: (*Limps into the room.*) Hello Dr. Cardinal.

HAROLD: (*Assists LAURA into a chair.*) Sit down, Mrs. Tatum, please. We don't want you on that foot any longer than necessary. Every unnecessary bit of pressure adds to the danger.

LAURA: Well, at least I have two feet. There are enough people around here with only one, or none from what I see in the waiting room. I don't want to end up like that. (*Pauses.*) Did you hear from Dr. Hargrove? Did he clear me for surgery?

HAROLD: (*Scowls.*) Yes. That's what I wanted to talk to you about. He called today to express his opinions.

LAURA: So can I undergo the surgery? It is still scheduled for tomorrow?

HAROLD: Yes, he did agree that you could undergo the surgery. That's the good news.

LAURA: And the bad news?

HAROLD: (*Leans forward.*) You have a bad doctor!

LAURA: Really?

HAROLD: Mrs. Tatum, may I call you Laura?

271

LAURA: Of course, although Dr. Hargrove always calls me Mrs. Tatum for some reason I've never understood. He never calls me Laura. I've always found that odd.

HAROLD: That's not the only thing odd about him. (*Pauses.*) Yes, he did clear you for surgery, as I said, but he told me I needed to amputate your foot.

LAURA: Amputate my foot? You mean cut it off entirely?

HAROLD: Yes.

LAURA: Why? Why would he say such a thing?

HAROLD: (*Again leans forward in confidence.*) I think he missed your diagnosis over a year ago and now he wants me to amputate your foot to get rid of the evidence of his mistake.

LAURA: Are you sure? Did he tell you that?

HAROLD: Well, he didn't exactly say it in those terms, but I have never had a doctor talk about amputation the way he did. He's a bad doctor, that's all. You'll need to find another one as soon as possible after the surgery.

LAURA: You really think my foot problem is something I had a year ago and Dr. Hargrove just missed it?

HAROLD: There's no doubt in my mind. Why else would he want me to amputate to get rid of the evidence?

LAURA: But an amputation, that's so brutal!

HAROLD: Yes, brutal and unreasonable.

LAURA: Is an amputation even a consideration?

HAROLD: Not in the least! I'm going to operate on you, of course, I will save your foot and you're going to do just fine. (*Pats LAURA on the shoulder.*) I'll take the very best possible care of you and we will save your foot together, regardless of what your personal doctor recommended.

LAURA: I'm in shock.

HAROLD: Yes, incompetence and deceit are shocking, aren't they?

LAURA: (*Pauses.*) Can I sue Dr. Hargrove?

HAROLD: (*Coyly.*) Of course you can and generally I would never suggest such a thing for one of my honored colleagues, but this really deviates from the standard of care. In your case, it might send a message as well as compensate you for your misery. (*Points to LAURA's foot.*) If this had been discovered earlier, you may not have even needed this surgery. Now look at your foot: collapsed, destroyed and dysfunctional. It's a real pity, a real avoidable catastrophe if only there had been a timely diagnosis. (*Pauses.*) Yes, in this case, litigation might send a much-needed and probably overdue message that such incompetence is not tolerated in the medical profession. Every doctor needs to be held to the highest moral and professional standards and sometimes, as we have here, it is clearly not the case. (*Points to LAURA's foot again.*) Now, back to your upcoming surgery.

LAURA: Please, Dr. Cardinal. I'm so upset I'm shaking.

HAROLD: (*Pats LAURA's shoulder.*) There, there. I understand. But calm down now so we can discuss your surgery. How do you feel?

LAURA: Nervous.

HAROLD: That's understandable. But I'm talking about your general health? Are you having any health issues I should know about?

LAURA: I guess I feel okay.

HAROLD: Do you have any reservations about the surgery?

LAURA: No! I may have had some before, but now I'm totally committed to the procedure. (*Leans in toward HAROLD.*) I have total faith in you and I'm full of gratitude to you for opening up my eyes. I've been blinded by Dr. Hargrove's personality, his cheerfulness, and his experience, but that's finished.

HAROLD: Knowledge is power, Laura. Sometimes it takes a second look from an outsider to rip away the veil of self-deception.

LAURA: Yes, yes. That's it, the veil of deception! I've been deceived, but now I see clearly. I've been blind, but now I see. It's all coming into focus. (*Pauses.*) Dr. Hargrove will pay! He will pay for hoodwinking me, for making me think he really cared about me. That's a crime; a real crime and it should be punished. And he will be punished, as God is my witness!

HAROLD: I'm just interested in your health and welfare, nothing more. I leave crime and punishment up to others. Now, let's get back to your surgery.

LAURA: All right, Doctor Cardinal.

HAROLD: Call me Harold, please.

LAURA: Okay, Harold.

HAROLD: We're a team, you and I, a team that will work together to restore you to optimal health, even if you will experience a reduction in functioning and activity level.

LAURA: Because of Dr. Hargrove's negligence.

HAROLD: I'll let you reach your own conclusions about that, Laura. Far be it from me to influence you in a legal issue.

LAURA: Of course, I respect your restraint and your professionalism. I'll be handling this in my own way after we finish with the surgery. And I feel fine, just mad as hell at being tricked and betrayed.

HAROLD: As well you should.

LAURA: Are you ready for tomorrow's surgery?

HAROLD: Perfectly! I appreciate your confidence and will work to justify it. I'll see you tomorrow at 6:30 a.m. at the surgery center. Remember, be fasting, and don't take your insulin. We don't want any hypoglycemia complicating things, do we?

LAURA: Thank you so much, Harold. Thank you for everything. I won't forget your kindness and consideration.

HAROLD: (*Bows slightly.*) Thank you. *A demain*!

LAURA: A de-man?

HAROLD: *A demain*, it's French for see you tomorrow.

LAURA: You're so cultivated. *Merci*! That's all the French I know.

HAROLD: That's plenty for me. Your gratitude is all I really want. Now, go get some sleep, we both want to be refreshed and rested for tomorrow's surgery.

(*Lights dim to dark.*)

SCENE II

(*JONATHAN DAVIS'S law office. There are a couple of chairs, perhaps a desk with a lamp, and maybe an oriental area rug. Nothing complex or fancy. He does have a large silver crucifix prominently placed on the wall. That is a necessary element.*)

LAURA: I want justice! No, I demand justice!

JONATHAN: And compensation?

LAURA: Of course! My life has been wrecked. I can't walk. I can't stand up to work! I have to use a cane to even get around the house! It's a crime!

JONATHAN: Malpractice is a civil offense, not a criminal matter.

LAURA: Not for me! It's a crime for a doctor to betray a patient's trust. I liked Dr. Hargrove. He took care of my family members. He chatted with me about all sorts of things. He seemed to care, and then he did this! (*Points to her feet.*) Two collapsed feet and a destroyed life.

JONATHAN: (*Taking notes.*) How did you get to me? Were you referred or did you see my ads?

LAURA: I asked around for a good lawyer and some people in our church had used you in the past. They said you were very competent and you got them what they deserved.

JONATHAN: Medical malpractice cases are not what I usually do. It's more personal injury and class action.

LAURA: (*Pointing to her feet again.*) And this isn't personal injury? Two bad feet caused by a doctor's negligence? (*Pauses.*) This is a no-brainer, Mr. Davis, a slam-dunk case, a done deal. Dr. Hargrove missed the diagnosis a year ago and then asked the surgeon to cut off my foot to get rid of the evidence. That's not just malpractice, that's criminal in my opinion.

JONATHAN: Cut off your foot? Get rid of the evidence? That sounds pretty extreme to me. How do you know this?

LAURA: Because Dr. Harold Cardinal, the orthopedic surgeon who operated on my foot, told me so. That's the surgeon I went to myself because my foot was getting worse and worse. I had to do something. And Dr. Cardinal said that Dr. Hargrove was so scared I'd find out he had missed the diagnosis for a year that he wanted the foot removed to get rid of the evidence.

JONATHAN: Did Dr. Hargrove say that to you directly?

LAURA: Of course not! But that doesn't surprise me. He was ashamed he had missed the diagnosis for a year and he never apologized or told me what happened. He just went behind my back to Dr. Cardinal and demanded an amputation. Can you imagine?

JONATHAN: It does seem awfully egregious. (*Pauses.*) Did you go back to Dr. Hargrove after the surgery?

LAURA: Back to Dr. Hargrove? Of course not! Why would I want to go back to a doctor that misdiagnosed and then betrayed me? No, never!

JONATHAN: (*Thoughtfully.*) You know I will have to do some research on this case. I will need Dr. Hargrove's records and Dr. Cardinal's and anyone else who has seen you. You will have to sign some releases.

LAURA: Yes, of course.

JOHATHAN: There's a lot of research that needs to be done prior to filing a lawsuit. And, of course, there's the medical review panel.

LAURA: What's that?

JONATHAN: That's a panel formed with three doctors, one from each attorney and one chosen by the two others that reviews the case to decide whether there was any "deviation from the standard of care."

LAURA: What does that mean?

JONATHAN: Deviation from the standard of care is just a fancy term for malpractice. (*Pauses.*) And they have to decide whether the deviation from care actually caused any harm, that's what we call a "tort."

LAURA: (*Holds up both legs with special shoes.*) Look at these! Look at these feet! They are both crushed. They're destroyed! I can't stand. I can't walk more than a few yards! And then I have to use this cane. You'd have to be blind to not see the damage. Of course there's harm. (*Pauses.*) Dr. Hargrove has destroyed my life by his incompetence. I want revenge! I want justice! I want compensation!

JONATHAN: And hopefully, we'll get all three in a big way.

LAURA: So you'll take my case?

JONATHAN: I think I can commit to you now, although sometimes a lot can change. It seems very straightforward, however.

LAURA: And the medical review panel? What if they disagree?

JONATHAN: No matter. Their decision is not binding. In your case, since it is so egregious, we can easily locate some very competent expert witnesses who will override the panel decision. The review panel is no more than a speed bump in the process. And if they happen to agree with you that there was deviation from the standard of care, it makes things so much easier. Dr. Hargrove's insurance company will be writing us a hefty check before the ink is dry on the panel's decision.

LAURA: (*Excited.*) Do it! Get the information. Start the process! The quicker we start, the quicker justice will be served. (*Grabs JONATHAN's sleeve.*) I believe in you. I believe in the justice system. You've got to help me punish Dr. Hargrove and get the justice and compensation I deserve! You've go to help me, Mr. Davis!

JONATHAN: And so I shall! (*Pat's LAURA's hand.*) We are in this together to the end. It will cost some time and money to invest in the case. And there will be the expensive expert witnesses. But that's just more of an investment in your future earnings and mine. Are you willing to make those investments?

LAURA: Anything!

JONATHAN: Even 40% of the eventual award?

LAURA: (*Surprised.*) Forty percent? That seems like so much. That might be a lot of money if I get the award I deserve.

JONATHAN: And well it might be. But that's the going rate, Mrs. Tatum.

LAURA: Laura.

JONATHAN: Laura, that's just how the system works. It allows people, such as you, with limited resources, to have full access to the justice system.

LAURA: And hourly fees? Does anyone do that?

JONATHAN: (*Laughs.*) Of course not! You would be bankrupt in a matter of weeks and I would be much less motivated to pursue your case. (*Pauses.*) Percentages of an eventual award solve all of the problems of access and create built-in incentives for the lawyer. Now let's get back to the case at hand and leave the theoretical considerations of contingency fees. When did Dr. Hargrove first miss the diagnosis?

LAURA: Well, it all started over a year ago. I came into to see Dr. Hargrove with swelling, lots of it for several weeks. And Dr. Hargrove didn't really know what it was. He was very upset and sent me to the hospital for some X-rays. I thought he X-rayed my foot, but he just did my thigh and leg. And he came to tell me the x-rays were negative.

JONATHAN: Then what?

LAURA: He sent me home and a few days later the swelling was still there, so he sent me to another local doctor for my veins. That doctor even wanted to operate on me.

JONATHAN: And did this other doctor find the diagnosis?

LAURA: He found something, but not the right diagnosis. He found something with the veins or something like that. He was the wrong kind of doctor, that's what Dr. Cardinal said.

JONATHAN: And after that?

LAURA: I still had let swelling and I called Dr. Hargrove to send me to a big center in Dallas that my family had used. They make diagnoses when no one else can.

JONATHAN: And they made the right diagnosis?

LAURA: No, they didn't because Dr. Hargrove sent me to the wrong kind of doctor there, too.

JONATHAN: So who finally did make the right diagnosis?

LAURA: Dr. Cardinal, the orthopedist in Dallas.

JONATHAN: How did you get to him?

LAURA: I went myself. Can you believe it? My neighbor saw me limping around and told me about this great foot doctor in Dallas. And that's when I finally got the right diagnosis and I got the truth . . .finally.

JONATHAN: So all the other doctors missed it, including Dr. Hargrove.

LAURA: Maybe, but they were the wrong kind of doctors. I don't blame them. I only blame Dr. Hargrove because he wanted to chop off my foot to get rid of the evidence. (*Holds up her feet.*) I want him punished! He shouldn't even be a doctor. I'm ashamed that me and my family ever went to him.

JONATHAN: Why did you?

LAURA: Because he had a good reputation. Little did I know it was all lies, lies and more lies, just a fancy façade hiding an evil and incompetent inside.

JONATHAN: (*Smiles.*) We'll get to the truth, Mrs. Tatum, Laura. We'll get to the truth and the truth shall set us free and bring justice and compensation in its wake. I swear to it!

LAURA: (*Grasps JONATHAN's hand.*) Oh, thank, you, Mr. Davis. Thank you Jonathan. I can hardly wait.

SCENE III (TEN YEARS LATER)

(*There is a raised platform on the stage with a solitary chair. This is the witness stand. The audience is the jury to which JONATHAN, DERRICK and LAURA both refer from time to time.*)

JONATHAN: So you went to Dr. Hargrove with a swollen right foot.

LAURA: Yes.

JONATHAN: And did he make the diagnosis at that time?

LAURA: No sir, it took him a year and then only when Dr. Cardinal already made the diagnosis.

JONATHAN: Show us you foot, please.

LAURA: The right one?

JONATHAN: Yes.

LAURA: Dr. Cardinal says this is something called a rocker foot because of the deformity. She how's there's no arch, but it comes down instead. (*Points to the bottom of her foot.*) It makes it hard to walk and it's very easy to get ulcers and other foot problems, too.

JONATHAN: Has this changed your life?

LAURA: Yes, of course. I can't walk, I can't work, I can't go on vacation, and I can't even go to social activities like church anymore. This has destroyed my life and could have been prevented.

JONATHAN: Thank you. (*Sits down in a chair by the side of the stage.*)

DERRICK: I'm Derrick Sharp and I represent Dr. Hargrove. Now, you say you went to Dr. Hargrove with a swollen foot.

LAURA: Yes, sir, I certainly did. My foot was red and hot and swollen.

DERRICK: And yet Dr. Hargrove's note shows that you complained of swelling to the whole right side of the body. Did you include the foot in your complaints?

LAURA: (*Sticks out her right foot.*) Yes, and now it's so damaged that I can barely walk, even with a cane. My life was ruined due to Dr. Hargrove's negligence. (*Starts to weep. Looks at the audience.*) Look at this foot! In fact, look at both of my feet! I used to have walks with my husband. I used to work in my garden. Now I can't even get up and around without a cane. (*Pauses.*) And Dr. Hargrove never even looked at my foot. He didn't even take off my shoe to examine me, but he wanted to chop off my foot later on.

DERRICK: (*Calmly.*) Let's look at the notes from Dr. Hargrove's visit on that date. (*Points to a page.*) Here is your very swollen thigh, and here is your swollen leg, but not nearly so much, and here is your foot with a little "plus one" and the word "edema" next to it. Do you know what that means?

LAURA: No.

DERRICK: It means that Dr. Hargrove had to push with his finger on the top of your foot to see if there was a little indentation. And he wrote that it was "plus one," because it can go up to "plus four" with a lot of edema.

LAURA: So?

DERRICK: So, Dr. Hargrove had to have taken off your shoes and had to have touched your foot. In fact, your own sworn deposition confirms it. (*Presents LAURA with a binder.*) Please read your response here.

LAURA: (*Reads.*) "Dr. Hargrove looked at my whole right side, including my thigh, my lower leg and my foot, which was a little swollen, but not nearly as much as my thigh. He even measured my thigh and leg with a measuring tape."

DERRICK: Thank you. (*Takes the binder.*) So your recent comments about Dr. Hargrove not examining your foot were mistaken?

LAURA: No! He never looked at my foot. My foot was swollen and red and hot! My foot was always the problem. Dr. Hargrove just missed it then and four months later when I went back to him.

DERRICK: Saying your foot was red, hot and swollen is in contradiction to your sworn testimony at your previous deposition. (*Pauses.*) When you went to the local specialist, the vein doctor, and then when you went to the specialty center in Dallas. . . .

LAURA: When I saw Dr. Cardinal?

DERRICK: No, the other specialist that Dr. Hargrove sent you to see, before you went to see Dr. Cardinal yourself.

LAURA: Yes.

DERRICK: Did you complain of your foot to either of those doctors?

LAURA: Of course, it was always the problem.

DERRICK: Are you sure, Mrs. Tatum?

LAURA: I am positive.

DERRICK: (*Puts the binder in front of LAURA.*) The question here in your deposition was. . . (*DERRICK reads*) "Why did you go to the specialist here locally and to the one in Dallas?" Please read your sworn response.

LAURA: "Because I was still complaining of swelling in the whole right side of my body."

DERRICK: The whole right side of the body?

LAURA: Yes, the body included the foot, unless someone chops it off, of course.

DERRICK: And yet we presented the records of both physicians, here and in Dallas, and there is NO mention of any complaints of the foot despite a complete exam by both doctors, which included an exam of both feet.

LAURA: They were mistaken.

DERRICK: Who's mistaken?

LAURA: They are!

DERRICK: You mean both doctors are mistaken and Dr. Hargrove was also mistaken despite what's documented in their charts, which corresponds with your sworn testimony?

LAURA: I guess so.

DERRICK: And is it possible that you are the one who is mistaken, Mrs. Tatum?

LAURA: No!

DERRICK: Isn't it possible that your memory of events has been distorted with the passage of over ten years of time? And isn't it possible that your self-deluded prevarications have become your own personal reality?

LAURA: What's a prevarication?

DERRICK: Lying.

LAURA: (*Yelling and standing up unsteadily.*) No! You're just playing lawyer tricks to get Dr. Hargrove off the hook. You're the one who's twisting the truth so I look like the guilty one! It's not so! It's just not so! (*Sits down.*)

DERRICK: (*Calmly.*) I can understand how your might become unclear about the events after ten years. (*Pauses.*) Sometimes I can't even remember what I ate for breakfast, and I'm quite a bit younger than you.

LAURA: (*Yells.*) I'm not senile! I'm not mistaken! And I'm not lying!

DERRICK: (*Calmly.*) Ten-year-old memories can bet muddled, don't you think? That's no crime.

LAURA: Maybe not, but it is a crime to misdiagnose someone and then try to get rid of the evident with an amputation.

DERRICK: (*Sternly.*) Did Dr. Hargrove say that to you? That he wanted to amputate your foot?

LAURA: No, but Dr. Cardinal said he did.

DERRICK: This is a hypothetical question, but why do your think Dr. Cardinal would say such a thing?

LAURA: Because it was the truth.

DERRICK: And this is also speculation, but perhaps Dr. Cardinal was angry with Dr. Hargrove for questioning the utility and safety of surgery on a very bad diabetic patient such as you? Maybe that questioning was more than Dr. Cardinal could tolerate, especially the day before the proposed surgery. Could that be an explanation, too?

LAURA: No!

DERRICK: No?

LAURA: No, because we have expert witnesses from Harvard that said that Dr. Hargrove missed the diagnosis a year earlier.

DERRICK: (*Sharply.*) And we have three expert witnesses who all disagree. And they have just as many qualifications and sometimes even more. (*Points to the audience, the "jury".*) So these good people, Dr. Hargrove's peers, will have to decide. (*Swings his arms to the audience.*) And let me remind you that there's not a doctor on this jury. In fact, only three jurors have a higher education. But let me also remind you that three physicians who sat on a medical review panel, certainly Dr. Hargrove's peers, all agreed that there was no malpractice, no deviation from the standard of care and no evidence of any kind of treatment but competent and compassionate care.

LAURA: (*Coolly.*) My attorney said they were mistaken.

DERRICK: So Dr. Hargrove, plus two specialists he sent you to, plus three physician medical review panelists, plus two eminent academic witnesses we retained are ALL mistaken about your diagnosis. But that you are the one who was right? Is that it, Mrs. Tatum?

LAURA: (*Looks a bit shaken.*) Yes, that's it. And our two expert witnesses are from Harvard.

DERRICK. Yes, from Harvard. And they are, indeed, highly qualified. But they did not have access to all of the records according to their own depositions.

LAURA: That's not my fault.

DERRICK: No, it's not. (*Pauses.*) Do you know how much an expert witness charges?

LAURA: How should I know that?

DERRICK: Between $500 and $700 an hour for around 24 hours of work. Three days of work on over 3,000 pages of evidence in this case. That's a cool $12,000 to $17,000 for their opinions. That's a lot of time and money, and yet there is not a shred of support for your allegations against Dr. Hargrove from our witnesses or the medical panel.

LAURA: I don't know anything about what experts charge or what they get.

DERRICK: No, you don't. And I strongly suspect that your attorney, Mr. Davis, has not shared that information with you.

LAURA: No.

DERRICK: Thank you for your testimony, Mrs. Tatum. I have no further questions.

LAURA: (*To DERRICK.*) Can you at least help me down from here?

DERRICK: Of course. (*Takes LAURA's hand and helps her down.*)

LAURA: (*Straightens up and pushes DERRICK away.*) I can make it from here. I've had enough of your help. (*Exits limping and using the cane.*)

(*Lights dim to dark.*)

SCENE IV (A FEW MINUTES LATER)

(*Small office with a couple of chairs. LAURA is seated and JONATHAN paces back and forth while talking.*)

JONATHAN: Laura, it's time to pull the plug on this case.

LAURA: Pull the plug?

JONATHAN: Yes, we need to end this trial, now!

LAURA: In the middle of the trial? The jury hasn't even heard all of the evidence?

JONATHAN: There are only two very strong defense witnesses left. It will only get worse for us, not better.

LAURA: We should at least let the trial go to the end. Let the jurors decide. Those jurors look like nice people.

JONATHAN: Nice or not, they can still tell when a witness has lied.

LAURA: Whose lying?

JONATHAN: Mr. Sharp, Dr. Hargrove's attorney, impeached you several times in case you did not notice.

LAURA: Impeached?

JONATHAN: Yes, he demonstrated that you had changed your story over time. You deviated from your previous sworn testimony in your deposition. In the juror's minds there is only one question, were you lying then or are you lying now? (*Pauses.*) We can't win. You've lost all credibility.

LAURA: Let's give it a try, anyway.

JONATHAN: Laura, I already got rid of any prospective jurors who were educated, or had nurses or doctors in their families, or who wouldn't sue their own doctors unless they were deliberately negligent. They were all eliminated! These are simple, poor, uneducated people, but they can understand when someone has lied.

LAURA: I didn't lie! I won't lie! It's a sin and God punishes sinners.

JONATHAN: Yes, and apparently he punishes their attorneys, too. (*Pauses.*) We must stop this trial now! I want to petition the court for a dismissal of this case so we can cut our losses.

LAURA: Our losses?

JONATHAN: My losses! Ten years of countless hours of legal work, $50,000 of expert witness testimony, $20,000 in other expenses. The days of travelling and depositions, motions, counter-motions, legal maneuvers. This has consumed my life for the last ten years.

LAURA: And mine? What about the impact this has had on me? Whose lawyer are you, anyway, mine or Dr. Hargrove's. You're going to let that negligent, lying, incompetent doctor go scot-free. He's going to walk out this courtroom on his two feet while I limp out on mine. It's not right!

JONATHAN: Has it occurred to you, Laura, that we just may have been wrong about this case?

LAURA: WRONG! By God, no! Dr. Cardinal told me to sue Dr. Hargrove.

JONATHAN: And where is Dr. Cardinal now?

LAURA: I don't know.

JONATHAN: I do. (*Pauses.*) He's retired. He retired the year after your case got started and moved to Costa Rica or heaven knows where else. He started this little ten-year forest fire and skipped town while everything burned down.

LAURA: Did he lie?

JONATHAN: I don't know. All I can tell you is that you swallowed his story, hook, line and sinker. I swallowed your story, hook, line and sinker. And that my distinguished Harvard expert witnesses also swallowed the story hook, line and sinker. And maybe, just maybe, it wasn't even true.

LAURA: No! I don't believe that Dr. Cardinal made it up. He told me the truth. He warned me. He said that a doctor like Dr. Hargrove shouldn't be practicing medicine because he was bad.

JONATHAN: He's not.

LAURA: What? Dr. Hargrove isn't bad?

JONATHAN: Didn't you listen? Dr. Hargrove left clinical practice and went into administrative medicine several years ago as some kind of administrative medical director.

LAURA: Good! Good for him. So we did win!

JONATHAN: Did we? Did his other patients win, too? Did the community win by losing a busy, well-respected physician who left clinical practice and went into paper pushing? Maybe he did more good than harm when he was taking care of folks, even you?

LAURA: I don't care! I don't care about the community or his other patients or what he thinks about me. (*Looks at JONATHAN.*) Go ahead, pull the plug! Stop the trial! I've already won.

JONATHAN: Did you? Did anyone? Maybe Dr. Hargrove's attorney did. He won a magnificent case and sent us packing with our tails between our legs. He earned a bucket load of money, so maybe he did win, but I didn't and you didn't and Dr. Hargrove didn't either.

LAURA: Don't mention that monster's name again in my presence. I hope he burns in hell where he belongs. I hope he suffered each and every day of these ten long years. I hope every one of his patients suffered when he left. It's just a fraction of what I suffered. (*Points to her feet.*) Look at these feet! Useless, painful, just waiting to flare up again.

JONATHAN: Maybe diabetes was the enemy all along, just like Mr. Sharp said. Maybe it's the disease and not Dr. Hargrove that was always the problem.

LAURA: (*Screams.*) Don't mention that man's name again or I'll fire you!

JONATHAN: And start over with a new lawyer for another decade? You know you'll have some court costs to pay now, don't you?

LAURA: No.

JONATHAN: You'll have to pay around $3,000 out of pocket, your pocket.

LAURA: You're kidding.

JONATHAN: No, I'm not.

LAURA: I lose, Dr. Hargrove walks free, and I still have to pay?

JONATHAN: That's better than the $100,000 of my legal labor and my out-of-pocket expenses. But I guess that doesn't matter to you, does it?

LAURA: (*Coolly.*) No, it doesn't. And you said no out-of-pocket expenses for me and you would get 40% of this huge settlement. That's what you said. (*Pauses.*) So I guess you lied, too.

JONATHAN: No, I didn't lie. But you did, Mrs. Tatum. You lied on the stand and sunk whatever was left of our sinking case.

LAURA: You lied! You lied, Dr. Cardinal lied, the experts lied and Dr. Hargrove lied. So where was the truth, Mr. hotshot lawyer? Where was the truth in these halls of justice?

JONATHAN: (*Swings his arms around in the air.*) There is no truth or justice here, only settlement. And this time there wasn't even any of that. (*Pauses.*) I suggest we go back into that courtroom and finish this drama.

LAURA: And if I refuse?

JONATHAN: You would have to fire me, assume all the court costs, and the bond for the physician panel, and a host of other costs. And then you would have to try and find another sucker lawyer and good luck with that. (*Reaches down and helps LAURA up.*) So I suggest we go in there and conclude this tragedy. (*Shakes his head as he leads LAURA off stage left.*)

(Lights dim. There is a solitary pool of light stage where DR. CARDINAL stands, dressed in a tropical print shirt and white pants. He is smiling and takes a swing at an imaginary golf ball. He yells "FORE!" loudly. Lights dim to dark.)

THE END

POLITICS AS USUAL

SPEECH WRITING

CIGARETTES AND CIVIL SURGEONS

GRAND CARITAS

SPEECH WRITING

CAST OF CHARACTERS

NATHAN WITHERSPOON: Politician, middle-aged. Speaks with presumed authority. Dressed in a white shirt and black pants and shoes, ageless in appearance.

DORA WANDERLUST: Nathan's lover. Voluptuous, pragmatic woman, dressed in a long skirt and peasant-like blouse. A retrograde hippy look.

HELEN WITHERSPOON: Nathan's wife. Dressed in an extravagant floor length dress, timeless and elegant in appearance.

SETTING

Stage is bare except for a simple chair in the middle. No suggestion of a specific time or place.

(*NATHAN stands in front of the empty chair and practices his speech. He holds a piece of paper that he may refer to from time to time. He gesticulates flamboyantly as he speaks.*)

NATHAN: My fellow citizens, my fellow patriots, we have reached a critical point in our history at which our very God-given rights are being trampled by an out-of-control federal government. We cannot allow this progressive erosion of liberty to continue. We have a constitutional right, even a moral obligation, to voice our indignation. (*Pauses.*) We cannot allow the blood that has been shed by our forefathers in the defense of liberty, which has soaked into our sacred soil, to have been shed in vain. (*Pauses. Looks at his note.*) Join me in opposing intrusions of this evil usurping authority into our beloved state. We are a nation of moral men and women with the duty to resist all evil, especially that which is foisted on us by our own so-called government. We must overcome this creeping immorality, this rot from above, that is corrupting men of good will everywhere, dragging us down into the moral morass of a Godless society.

DORA: (*Knocks on a side door and peaks in.*) Nathan? Nathan Witherspoon? Is that you?

NATHAN: (*Looks at DORA in surprised recognition.*) Dora!

DORA: (*Comes in. Looks around to make sure there is no one else.*) Yes. It's me and I'm so glad to see you.

NATHAN: What in the hell are you doing here! You can't be seen here by anyone. My wife might arrive at any minute.

DORA: (*Looks around again.*) Well, she's not here yet and I need to talk to you.

NATHAN: Make it fast! I have thing to do, people to meet and a campaign to run. Say what you have to say and then get out.

DORA: (*Approaches NATHAN and seductively caresses his cheek.*) That's an awfully cold reception from a man who called me the prettiest young thing he had ever seen in or out of clothing.

NATHAN: (*Pulls her hand off and backs away.*) That was a long time ago, an error of youth, a lapse in moral values, a slip of the. . . . (*pauses.*)

DORA: The tongue? And a little more than that if my memory serves me right. You little devil you. (*Tweaks NATHAN's cheek.*)

NATHAN: (*Pulls away and points to the door.*) Get out! Get out of here and don't every come back. If you think you're going to blackmail me for political or financial reasons, you are sadly mistaken, you little whore!

DORA: Just a minute, Don Juan! Before you get up on your moral high horse, I thought your might want to look at this. (*Pulls a photo out of a little handbag. Shows it for NATHAN.*)

NATHAN: Who's that?

DORA: Your son, of course. He's six years old and as smart as a whip.

NATHAN: You're lying.

DORA: No, I'm not. He's had a DNA test and if you would be so kind as to give me a bit of your saliva, we can straighten this out in a couple of weeks.

NATHAN: I will not! And you can't make me either.

DORA: Maybe I can't, but a judge might be able to. (*Pauses.*) Do you really want that much publicity? (*Pauses and replaces the picture.*) I just want some decent child support and a fat 529 educational fund for his college expenses. Is that too much to ask of a father?

HELEN: (*Knocks at the door.*) Hello! Nathan, are you in there? I thought I heard voices.

NATHAN: (*Signals to DORA to sit in the chair.*) Just practicing my speech.

HELEN: (*Comes in wearing a very beautiful and extravagant full-length gown. Glances briefly at DORA and then back to NATHAN.*) How do you like it? (*Looks back at DORA.*) Who's this?

NATHAN: A former acquaintance. She's listening to my speech.

HELEN: (*Bows in DORA's direction.*) Nice to meet you. A friend of Nathan's is a friend of mine. (*Turns in front of NATHAN and DORA.*) Do you really like it, Nathan? Really?

NATHAN: (*Shrugs his shoulders.*) It's okay. I've got other things on my mind.

HELEN: (*To DORA.*) Well, what do you think of it? Woman-to-woman?

DORA: It's very nice. A bit retro, but also timeless. What's the occasion?

HELEN: The Presidential Ball next month. I want to make a real fashion statement.

DORA: It's really beautiful. You will need some accessories, of course.

HELEN: Of course! I was thinking of an Italian beaded purse and some understated French jewelry with a smattering of diamonds.

DORA: Naturally.

HELEN: (*To DORA.*) So how long have you known Nathan? A former acquaintance did you say?

DORA: Yes, a former acquaintance from six years ago and a little more.

NATHAN: (*Yells.*) Dora! That's enough! You need to get out right now or I'll call the police to drag you out of here.

HELEN: Nathan! That's a very unkind way to treat an old friend.

NATHAN: (*To HELEN.*) Stay out of this! This woman needs to leave. She's a tramp and a blackmailer.

DORA: And the mother of your son!

(*An embarrassed silence follows.*)

NATHAN: Get out!

DORA: If that's the way you want it. Perhaps a subpoena will help you clear your head. All I need is a mouth swab to establish paternity. (*Swings a swab around in the air.*)

HELEN: (*Looking back and forth. Speaks to DORA.*) The mother of your son?

DORA: (*Pulls out the picture.*) Yes! Here's the picture. He's six years old now and your husband hasn't paid a dime of child support. Of course he didn't know until today. But it's never too late to do the right thing.

HELEN: (*Looks at the picture.*) Cute boy. What's his name?

DORA: Bradley.

HELEN: He does have Nathan's eyes. (*Looks back at NATHAN.*) And his hair.

DORA: And his genes.

HELEN: (*To NATHAN.*) Is this true?

NATHAN: She's lying. She's a lying gold-digger and. . . .

HELEN: And the mother of your child. (*Pauses. Speaks to DORA.*) What is your name?

DORA: Dora Wanderlust.

HELEN: Stage name?

DORA: No, it's the real one. My grandfather was German.

HELEN: That's odd, so was mine. He was a Vandenberg from the Rhineland somewhere, or was it Alsace-Lorraine? Oh well. (*To DORA.*) So what are you looking for, Ms. Wunderlust.

NATHAN: Helen, stop this minute!

HELEN: Stop? Why? So you can make this scandal blow up in our faces. And I get dragged into this drama as the supportive wife of a philandering prick politician, another one. Is that what you really want, you fool!

NATHAN: No, of course not, but I don't want to be blackmailed by this tramp.

HELEN: (*Back to DORA.*) So what exactly do you want, my dear?

DORA: Child support until Bradley is 21 and a 529 for his college education.

HELEN: How much?

DORA: A thousand dollars a month in child support and two hundred thousand in a 529.

HELEN: How about $850 a month and a hundred and fifty thousand in the 529?

NATHAN: You're both crazy!

HELEN and DORA: (*To NATHAN.*) Shut up!

DORA: Okay, $900 a month and a $175,000 in the 529.

HELEN: (*Reaches out her hand.*) Deal!

DORA: (*Takes HELEN's hand and shakes it.*) Deal!

NATHAN: I'm not submitting this this.

HELEN: (*Pushes NATHAN back into the chair and sits him down.*) Of course you are. A political career, tainted by sexual scandal, means tedious questions, endless enquires and costly legal battles. Everyone will want to know all the details about Miss Wunderlust. . . .

DORA: Wanderlust.

HELEN: Wanderlust, excuse me. (*To NATHAN.*) You pay her what your need to pay and then she goes away. (*To DORA.*) You will be going away, won't you and remaining perfectly silent?

DORA: Of course. What kind of a woman do you think I am anyway?

HELEN: (*Nods. To NATHAN.*) Miss Wanderlust and your son, Bradley, both go away and you can continue your incredible political assent while I continue my astonishing social one at your side.

NATHAN: That's raw hypocrisy.

HELEN: I'm a hypocrite and you are not? You and your so-called family values and fiscal conservatism! You and your God-given individual and state liberties in the face of despotic Washington evil! You think that's not hypocritical, you with your God-given right to fornicate anywhere and with whomever you please? (*Turns to DORA.*) Can I see that photo again?

DORA: Sure. (*Pulls out the picture.*)

HELEN: He's very cute. Is he really smart?

DORA: Oh yes. He spoke at two and already reads very good at six.

HELEN: Well. He reads very well.

DORA: Sorry. Reads very well.

HELEN: Have your considered Harvard? All Nathan's family went to Harvard. The all became all lawyers, mostly sleazy plaintiffs' attorneys and a smattering of politicians.

DORA: I think I prefer Princeton.

HELEN: Really? Princeton just doesn't have Harvard's cachet even though it's a very good university. (*Pauses.*) Do you think $175,000 will be enough in that 529 for either of those schools? You know those fancy Eastern schools hardly ever give any scholarships.

NATHAN: Helen! For heaven's sake.

HELEN: Shut up!

DORA: I hope so. What with compounded interest and dividend re-investment over the next 12 years, Bradley's 529 might be worth over half a million with the right funds. Even with inflation, that ought to be more than enough.

HELEN: (*Takes DORA by the arm.*) Do you have time for lunch?

DORA: (*Looks at her watch.*) Well, if it's not too long. I have to be back at work by two. (*Looks at the swab in her hand.*) And will I be needing this?

HELEN: Oh no, dear. I believe you and your child's looks are a dead giveaway. (*Pauses.*) Where do you work again?

DORA: Over at the NSA, I'm a secretary, but I do the most fascinating work with classified information.

HELEN: Very interesting. (*Leads DORA toward the door.*) We have the most charming financial planner, a very attractive young man. I'm sure he might be willing to work with you and Bradley. (*Looks at her dress.*) I will have to change, of course, but that should just take a minute.

NATHAN: What about me?

HELEN: Just keep working on that speech. I'm sure your colleagues will be impressed. If it's good enough, it might get onto social media or Fox Network or something. The President might even take a look at it.

DORA: Do you know the President?

HELEN: Of course we do, and his wife, too. She's such a charming woman, so pleasant and down-to-earth. And her husband is the model of fidelity, or so I'm told. (*To DORA.*) Do you have a boyfriend?

DORA: Oh yes, a nice young man that also works in data, a Mr. Snowden, Edward Snowden.

HELEN: Is he trustworthy?

DORA: Oh yes, I would trust him with my life.

HELEN: Just like Nathan, eh?

DORA: (*Laughs.*) I hope it works out better than with him.

> (*DORA and HELEN laugh. The women leave. NATHAN puts his head in his hands. The paper with his speech drops to the floor. NATHAN shakes his head.*)

THE END

CIGARETTES AND CIVIL SERVANTS

CAST OF CHARACTERS

SULTAN: He can be richly dressed or just wear a turban of some sort to denote his status as Sultan. Costuming can be just about anything, from subdued to over the top. He is imperious and overbearing. His speech drips with condescension and pretentiousness.

VIZIER: He is also either simply or richly dressed, depending on the desire of the director. He is obsequious and fawning, but with an obvious intelligence and a definite survival instinct. He is holding a piece of PVC pipe that looks like a large cigarette. He also has a computer list and an invitation on a small table as well.

SETTING

The setting should contain an elevated throne or something of that sort, either stylized or lavish, depending on time and resources. The stage can have a few props to suggest the royal court, but nothing is absolutely necessary.

(*The SULTAN is seated in his throne and awaits the VIZIER, who presents the SULTAN with a piece of PVC pipe in the form of a giant cigarette.*)

SULTAN: And what do you propose to me today, oh Grand Vizier?

VIZIER: (*Holds an over-sized cigarette and presents it to the SULTAN as he bows.*) This, Your Highness.

SULTAN: (*Frowns.*) What is it?

VIZIER: It is an oversized cigarette, the symbol of a potential source of great wealth for your administration.

SULTAN: Oh, come now! Even the least of our citizens knows that tobacco causes lung cancer and increases medical costs, which we pay for out of the state coffers. We should probably just outlaw the nasty things.

VIZIER: Oh yes, Your Highness. It is reported that several thousand of your citizens die each year prematurely from smoking and from second-hand smoke as well.

SULTAN: Yes and each death is a tragedy, the loss of a taxpayer. Yet it must be said that premature death in the right age group reduces social security payments that need to be paid. That is an indirect benefit, isn't it? Didn't they demonstrate that in study in Bohemia?

VIZIER: Quite so, Your Grace. And that is a silver lining to the national tragedy of tobacco related deaths. (*Holds the cigarette up again.*) But premature deaths only help with the Imperial debt, not our Provincial debt. (*Pauses.*) What we need is not to outlaw cigarettes, but to increase the tax on them to help fill our provincial coffers. We could double it! Triple it! For every increase in taxes, there is a corresponding decrease in the number of smokers and a huge windfall for the provincial treasury. (*Holds the cigarette up in triumph.*) Everyone wins! You get more money, less people smoke, and the cost of medical care goes down. It's brilliant!

SULTAN: (*Waves his hands in the air.*) No, no, no! A thousand times no!

VIZIER: (*Lets the cigarette slump down.*) Your Greatness, what is the matter? This is a win-win situation for you and your citizens! Triple the tax and stabilize the budget and save lives! (*Swings the cigarette around in the air.*)

SULTAN: (*Grabs the cigarette and strikes the VIZIER.*) You fool! Have you understood nothing? (*Continues to strike.*) You must not say the "T" word!

VIZIER: Triple? Well then let's just double it, Your Highness.

309

SULTAN: (*Strikes the VIZIER a number of times.*) NO, FOOL! (*Screams.*) TAX! (*Continues to beat the VIZIER, chasing him around the stage.*) I promised the people no taxes and what you propose now would clearly be a tax.

VIZIER: (*Cringes.*) It's just a renewal. A small tax already exists. Renewal starts with a "R," Oh Sublime One.

SULTAN: (*Beats the VIZIER again.*) The people are not complete fools. I promised fewer taxes, less government and more jobs. Tell me how a cigarette tax fits in with my promises?

VIZIER: It's just a small tax, with a small "t."

SULTAN: Shut up! (*Strikes the VIZIER again.*) Do you think I want to remain a provincial Sultan for the rest of my life?

VIZIER: (*Bows respectfully.*) No, Oh Great One.

SULTAN: Of course not! I have much higher political ambitions than to remain in this God-forsaken wilderness for the rest of my life. (*Pauses.*) And the key to my continued political advancement is ideological purity.

VIZIER: But you are very pure, Oh Beloved One. You are the purist of the pure.

SULTAN: Yes, you are right, God be praised. I am as pure as the new born lamb, the freshly fallen snow, the lily of the valley. (*Turns on the VIZIER.*) And it is my intention and it should be your goal to keep me that way.

VIZIER: Of course, Your Highness. How foolish of me to have brought up such a silly idea.

SULTAN: Yes, it was a silly idea. Now get that cigarette out of my sight before I beat you to death with it.

(*VIZIER puts the cigarette away and returns with a stack of computer paper.*)

SULTAN: I hope you have something more useful this time.

VIZIER: (*Bows and begins to unroll the reams of computer paper. It can also be a long scroll of some sort.*) This is the current list of your civil servants that you requested, Your Grace.

SULTAN: (*Looks at the list. Grabs it and tears it in half.*) There! I have torn it in half. Fire all of them on this half of the list. (*Hands half of the list to the VIZIER.*) The others can stay for the time being.

VIZER: (*Looks distressed.*) You Highness, you have some loyal and trusted civil servants on this half of the list. And our province has terrible problems of poverty, illness and ignorance that they are trying to address.

SULTAN: (*Screaming.*) These civil servants are parasites off the provincial purse! These so-called public servants are part of the problem, not part of the solution. Any fool can see that.

VIZIER: But Your Grace, who will heal the poorest of the poor or teach the most disadvantaged children? You yourself have said that education and healthcare are the roads to prosperity.

SULTAN: Yes, education and healthcare are the roads to prosperity. And we are among the poorest and unhealthiest of the Imperial Provinces. But the poor, we shall always have among us, as a Prophet has said. And increasing the financial burden on our Province by these blood-sucking civil servants, bloated with their pensions and their excessive leave and early retirements, is NOT the solution. (*Swings the list around.*) These parasites must go!

VIZIER: But the poorest of the poor, Your Grace?

SULTAN: Let them pull themselves up by their bootstraps!

VIZIER: Your Highness, thirty percent of the population has no shoes, much less boots.

SULTAN: (*Strikes the VIZIER.*) Impudent fool! Why do you torture me with such details? (*Throws the list at him.*) Get rid of all this dead weight! (*Pauses.*) We will start a public service campaign about the merits of self-reliance, self-education, and healthier life-style choices. (*Pauses.*) It cannot be the responsibility of the state to support everyone. We are here to create a healthy economic environment and a level playing field for all of the citizens.

VIZIER: Your Highness, your own family was of humble immigrant origin. You are indeed living proof of the ability of the meek to rise to the highest level of the state. Of course you are correct in your assessment. (*Bows.*)

SULTAN: Yes, you are right. But you are not right that I am at the highest level of the state. (*Pauses.*) Do you have any other important issues?

VIZIER: One last detail, Your Exalted One.

SULTAN: Be quick. I must go and do my spiritual duties at the temple.

VIZIER: (*Hands the SULTAN an oversized invitation.*) The Emperor has requested your presence in the Imperial Capital at a royal reception.

SULTAN: (*Takes the invitation and looks at it.*) It's already next week.

VIZIER: Yes, next week, Oh Sublime One.

SULTAN: Send the Emperor a note and tell him I am in ill health and cannot attend.

VIZIER: What illness, Your Highness?

SULTAN: What does it matter? It's my private health information, isn't it? That's protected by Imperial Law and he doesn't need to know.

VIZIER: Perhaps private health information is protected for regular citizens, but I suspect the Emperor may want to know if one of his Provincial sultans is seriously ill. Refusing to furnish information might be viewed as impertinent, Your Grace, or even treasonous.

SULTAN: Impertinent, eh? Treasonous, eh? Well let it be known that I am suffering from recurrent bronchitis secondary to tobacco use. How about that?

VIZIER: Do you smoke, Your Highness?

SULTAN: Of course not, it's a dirty, dangerous habit.

VIZIER: And if the Emperor should know that you don't smoke, what then, Your Grace?

SULTAN: My future destiny does not lie in slavish obedience to the Emperor. My power comes from the people of this province, who love and support me. They know that I suffer with them and bleed with them. They know I try and lighten their tax burden. When I got to the temples, the crowds throng around me and call out my name. (*Pauses.*) With a little luck and a lot of skill, I can please the other provincial sultans, who share my beliefs. We can refuse Imperial Diktats and I will be respected and even glorified by everyone, except perhaps the civil servants. And what of them? (*Pauses.*) I cannot be expected to bow to every whim of the Imperial Ding-Dong in the capital, which is located, I might add, many thousands of miles away.

VIZIER: Open confrontation with the Emperor seems dangerous, My Lord.

SULTAN: Yes, you are right. Open rebellion has been punished cruelly in the past. Our Province has suffered destruction and indignity at the hands of Imperial occupiers many decades ago. That, however, is the past, Praise be to God! (*Pauses.*) This is the present, however, and it is different. We need only drag our feet, evoke problems of implementation and logistics about Imperial Diktats. The time will come when we have a new Emperor, one that recognizes the wisdom of my philosophies. (*Pauses.*) Then, who knows, perhaps I will be exalted and transferred to the Imperial Capital?

VIZIER: The Imperial Capital, which you call so painfully out of touch with the provinces, Your Highness? Is that really your goal?

SULTAN: (*Ignores the comment. Gives the VIZIER a nasty look.*) Or maybe I will be elected as the new Emperor myself after the demise of the current usurper.

VIZIER: Dangerous words, Your Grace. (*Looks around.*) You never know who may be listening.

SULTAN: (*Hands the invitation back to the VIZIER.*) On second thought, I shall attend. I will be able to assess the political climate of the Imperial Capital and meet with those who share my ideas. (*Claps his hands.*) Vizier!

VIZIER: Yes, Your Highness.

SULTAN: I will attend and I must be radiant. I want to have the finest clothing that money can buy. I need to dazzle them all with the sheer brilliance of it.

VIZIER: Yes, Your Grace.

SULTAN: Send for those two new tailors who came from the Imperial Capital. I have heard it said they could make clothes that only a worthy

314

ruler can see. (*Spins around.*) I will be dressed in such a magnificent style that all the people in the Capital will recognize me for my merits as a ruler. It must be the finest that money can buy. Spare no expense. It will be fit for a future Emperor.

VIZIER: Yes, My Lord, I have heard these are remarkable tailors, indeed, intelligent and skillful beyond belief. (*Pauses.*) But then again, what is beyond belief may not be believable. Caution is always a prudent course with people we do not know.

SULTAN: (*Screams.*) Caution! You fool. There is no caution in the pursuit of the truly remarkable. Let me be the judge of excellence in policy as well as wardrobe. Do I make myself understood!

VIZIER: (*Bows.*) Of course, My Lord. How foolish of me. I will find these men and send them to you at once.

SULTAN: (*Returns to the throne and picks up a mirror.*) Yes, indeed. I will dazzle them all in the Capital. Just another step in my progression to where destiny has called me. I can't wait for those tailors to make me something that truly reveals the depths of my inner beauty. Something only the most worthy ruler and most worthy citizens can behold. (*Spins around with his robe swinging out and his arms extended in the air.*) I can see it now! So beautiful, so extraordinary, so captivating, so ME. (*Clutches his hands to his chest and bows his head in self-admiration.*)

(*Lights dim to dark.*)

THE END

GRAND CARITAS

CAST OF CHARACTERS

HUBERT: Governor of a Southern state. Politician with a vision. Speaks with a pronounced Southern rural accent and may be overweight. Dressed in a 30's style white linen suit and flat-topped straw hat.

EDDIE LE BLANC: Assistant to Hubert. Speaks with a pronounced Southern accent with Cajun intonations. He is dressed simply, perhaps in some sort of uniform.

DR. FRED SAGE: Speaks with a slight Southern accent. His grammar and pronunciation are both correct. He is impeccably dressed in a suit and tie from the 30's.

MARTY: Governor of a Southern state. The character needs to be slender, well dressed. His speaks correctly, almost as if English is his second language. Dressed in a contemporary fitted suit, obviously of good quality.

TONY: Works with Governor in Scene II. May be the same actor as Eddie LeBlanc, but he speaks without a Southern accent. He is well dressed, but casual, perhaps a sports coat and tie.

DR. CARL PEACH: Well-dressed in a contemporary suit and tie. Well-spoken younger man without a regional accent.

SETTING

Both scenes have minimal, if any set items. There should be an American flag that denote an official event or location in the first two scenes. If it is not clear about the date, there may be a sign marked "1930" for Scene I and "2012" for Scene II.

Scene III should be totally empty, with no suggestion of time or place.

SCENE I – LE DEBUT (THE BEGINNING) (1932)

HUBERT: (*Waves his hands in the air and looks around.*) Can you see it, Eddie?

EDDIE: (*Looks around.*) No, boss.

HUBERT: That's cuz you ain't no visionary like me.

EDDIE: What's a visionary?

HUBERT: Someone who can see the future before it happens just by usin' their imagination.

EDDIE: No, I guess, I ain't no visionary. I'm just a downed to earth country boy with a sixth grade education, hardly any book learnin' at all.

HUBERT: That's the problem. (*Slaps EDDIE on the back.*) You never got the benefits of a decent education and I'm goin' change all that.

EDDIE: Boss, we done heard all it all before. Every politician promises the little folks books and roads and doctorin' and then they pockets the state money and hightails it out of the country before they can git caught.

HUBERT: I'm different.

EDDIE: (*Looks skeptical.*) Really?

HUBERT: I really am different. I come from the backcountry, too, them piney woods up North. I know poverty and even hunger. But I got myself through law school and got enough book learning to be elected governor. (*Pauses.*) I wasn't easy, no sireebob. I done struggled for every scrap of information and every vote I ever got. (*Pauses.*) But once the power and money started to cumulate, then it jus' snowballed. More power, more votes, more money. (*Pauses.*) It's been a wild ride to the top and now y'all, the people, are goin' benefit from my rise to the top. (*Swings his arms around.*) We goin' build the biggest, the best hospital, and fill it with the smartest doctors in the entire South. I'm goin' fill it with the best professors that money can buy from all of them fancy Eastern schools. It's goin' have the best, shiniest equipment in the country. Yesiree, the best that money can buy!

EDDIE: Whose money? Not the taxpayers, I hope.

HUBERT: No, course not, Standard Oil's money, and lots of it. Those fat cats have been rapin' this state and stealin' us blind. If I could I'd nationalize them sons-of-bitches, but that ain't goin' happen anytime soon. Gotta respect free enterprise and all that.

EDDIE: Them oil companies; they'd just git up and leave and never come back if you taxes 'em like that.

HUBERT: (*Laughs.*) No, they won't. They ain't goin' nowhere and neither is that oil. They'd squeak and squawk and whine all the way up to Washington D.C. and Wall Street. But in the end, it won't make a damn bit of difference. They gotta come back and take that oil where they can find it and pay a hell of lot more to take it out.

EDDIE: Do you really think it's possible?

HUBERT: Possible? It's goin' happen just like this hospital is goin' happen. (*Pauses.*) Grand Caritas Hospital will be the first of many. We can't neglect them poor folks around the rest of the state. We gotta think about every corner of this god-damned state! They'll all get their new hospitals. (*Pauses.*) Maybe not in my lifetime or yours, but sometime in the future it'll happen. By God, it will happen. (*Grabs EDDIE.*) We don't have to be the clo-a-ca of the nation, the laughin' stock of them Eastern prep school snobs, them rich bastards with their stock coupons and houses in the Hamptons. We don't have to be the bottom of the barrel for everythin' with all them barrels of oil gettin' pumped out day after day, year after year. No, we're goin' be the top o' the barrel now.

EDDIE: What's a clo-a-ca?

HUBERT: That's a body part of a chicken. (*Sees DR. SAGE coming.*) Never mind. (*Walks over to DR. SAGE and shakes his hand.*) Glad you could make it, doc.

DR. SAGE: Good to see you, sir. Sorry I was late. We had a little emergency at the hospital. So what did you want me to see?

HUBERT: (*Waves his hands around and points to the distance.*) There, over there. That's gonna be the new Grand Cartias Hospital, the biggest and the best hospital in all the South. You gotta believe me, doc. (*Takes DR. SAGE by the shoulders.*) This project is goin' happen and it's goin' be so good and so solid that it will still be here in a 1,000 years. Yup, the thousand year Grand Caritas Hospital! It'll be a testimony to dedicated staff and a fine administrator like you. Dr. Sage, you gotta help me make this happen. And it's gonna happen because I'm one son-of-a-bitch determined politician and the people want it, too. Them grateful citizens are goin' love the place and wanna vote for someone who finally shows he really cares about 'em.

DR. SAGE: Be careful, Governor, you have enemies out there in industry and finance. Wall Street and the White House aren't very excited about your schemes down here in Louisiana. The President thinks you may have just gotten too big for your political britches. Megalomonaical is the term I've heard him use.

HUBERT: (*Pronounces each syllable.*) Mego-al-o-man-ia-cal? What does it mean?

DR. SAGE: Delusions of grandeur from a mental disorder. And frankly, I'm not sure it would be a favorable career goal for me to associate with a project that hasn't even left the planning stage. That's just a big, muddy field over there. I'm sure you understand my reticence.

HUBERT: (*Explodes.*) Whose side are you on, anyway, doc?

DR. SAGE: Yours, of course, sir. I want to see the Caritas Hospital materialize and be the site of a world-class medical school. I want it to be a source of knowledge and medical care for the poor of this state who have nothing, no money, no insurance, not even good health. You are a visionary, sir. I just need to be prudent.

HUBERT: (*Calms.*) Of course, I do understand. And I do appreciate your support. (*Pauses.*) Schools, roads, books, vaccinations, all paid for by the largess of Standard Oil and them other oil companies. They just won't be able to say no to me. They'll line up with the money in checks and suitcases filled with cash and Grand Caritas Hospital will become a reality. (*Pauses. Slaps DR. SAGE on the back.*) And don't forget all that support from them civil servants of mine. I got their deducts to help fund my campaigns. And what with the poor folks, includin' them votin' Negroes, you'll see this buildin' rise from that mud to become a gleamin' monument to me and medicine, the New Jerusalem of learnin' and healin' right here in this amazin' city.

EDDIE: (*Claps.*) You tell 'em, boss!

DR. SAGE: Astonishing.

HUBERT: Yes, astonishing. (*Slaps DR. SAGE on the back.*) And you, doc, are goin' head up this great institution. You are goin' see the building rise up brick by brick from this swampy soil to become a world-class medical institution, so help me God.

DR. SAGE: I'm not sure I'm up for the task. It's monumental.

HUBERT: Of course you are, doc. (*Turns to EDDIE.*) Don't you think doc's up for it?

EDDIE: Damn right!

HUBERT: (*To DR. SAGE.*) Yes, sir, even if you're related to that scoundrel of judge that gives the boss so much trouble.

DR. SAGE: Don't go there, Governor, please.

HUBERT: (*To DR. SAGE.*) Of course, let's just let bygones be bygones. A few harsh words spoken in haste and anger from your father-in-law can't keep us from workin' together, can they, doc?

DR. SAGE: No, they shouldn't. Not between gentlemen, anyway, both working for the better health of the people of this state.

HUBERT: Yeah, gentlemen. (*Takes DR. SAGE by the shoulder and escorts him off stage.*) So you go along, doc, and start recruitin' faculty from every distinguished medical school in the country. And remember, spare no expense! We want the talent and the brains to run this place. And I don't give a damn how much Standard Oil is goin' to pay for it.

DR. SAGE: Thanks. I will do my best, sir. You won't regret it. (*Exits.*)

HUBERT: (*To EDDIE.*) Now you make sure that the doctor's father-in-law, that sleazy, no good, son-of-bitch judge, gits what he deserves. You tell them over in the Picayune about his affair with that Creole bitch down in Opelousas. And don't spare any of the lurid details. I'm sorry for the doc, but that asshole father-in-law of his has gotta go.

EDDIE: Sure thing, boss. (*Exits.*)

HUBERT: (*Turns around. Waves his hands in the air.*) It will be a triumph, a perfect success. I will get my glory with the poor, who'll get the hospital they deserve. And Standard Oil gets what they deserve for tryin' to suck this state dry and throw us away on the garbage. Now that's real charity for you, takin' from the undeservin' rich and givin' to the deservin' poor. I can see it now, by God, I can see it! (*Exits.*)

SCENE II – LE DEMANTALEMENT (THE DISMANTELING) (2012)

MARTY: The poor! You really think this monstrous system is serving the poor?

TONY: Sir, the press is crucifying you for dismantling the state run healthcare system. They say your have no room in your heart for charity.

MARTY: Charity? For whom? For the blood-sucking civil servants who work in it? For the vendors who sell to it? For the people who get second rate medical care in an expensive and antiquated system? Is that what you call charity? We've spent billions over the years? And for what? To be the laughing stock of the Union, the cloaca of the nation? The last in health care over and over again.

TONY: We just don't have the private infrastructure to take on the task of caring for the poor. There are too many sick, indigent people in this state.

MARTY: Sick and poor, yes. And too many, yes. You know what Jesus said?

TONY: He said lots of things.

MARTY: "The poor you shall always have among you." But those are not the people on which to found a prosperous state. We need to rely on private entrepreneurship, private practices and personal responsibility to pull us out of this morass into which we have sunk over the decades.

TONY: Perhaps with federal help, it might be possible.

MARTY: Federal help? Are you crazy? If we ask for federal help, we sacrifice any ideological credibility we might still possess. Can't you smell the hypocrisy of it all? On the one hand, we râle against the excesses of federal government and on the other hand, we take federal handouts in the vain hope that we can somehow spend our way to prosperity and health. There's no way federal assistance can help us. Besides, it will completely sabotage my conservative credentials.

TONY: It's impossible otherwise, sir. The poor don't have the time, money or transportation to get care now, much less if we don't have a safety net system. We're already 48th out of 50 states in our health rankings. How much lower can we get?

MARTY: 50th! We can still sink to 50th! And the sick and poor can go elsewhere for help or die in the streets and decrease the excess population.

TONY: That's harsh, sir, even for you. (*Pauses.*) My brother had a streak of bad luck and if it weren't for the state run health system, he would have died, too. He spent almost a month in the ICU. He got good care, too. Without Grand Caritas Hospital, he would have died.

MARTY: I'm sorry for your brother. I'm sorry for everyone's brothers and sisters who are sick and poor and uninsured. But you cannot buy good health, especially with a separate-but-unequal system, born out of the erroneous beliefs of a populist demagogue. (*Pauses.*) It's done! That era is finished. And the ghosts of its creator and all of his like minded believers should stay down in their graves where they belong. (*Points downward.*)

TONY: Dr. Peach is here to see you, sir. He's been waiting outside over an hour.

MARTY: Show him in, please.

DR. PEACH: Thank you for seeing me, Governor. I hope you have some good news about hospital funding.

MARTY: Dr. Peach, you are a fine, dedicated physician, with a wealth of knowledge and a reputation for personal integrity. But you must realize you are on the wrong side of history. There will be no more funding for the state medical system at this time. It's finished!

DR. PEACH: Sir, there are no viable private alternatives to the state run health system at this time. The private sector is neither interested in nor obliged to see the hordes of poor, sick people that live in this state. They're over 45% of the population.

MARTY: (*Menacingly.*) Doctor, don't lecture me on statistics in this state. I know them all by heart. And you should know that we have dumped billions of dollars down the rat hole of state-delivered medical care and our health outcomes are abysmal. You should know better than me that insanity is doing the same thing over and over again despite catastrophic results. My predecessors may have been insane, but I am not.

DR. PEACH: University Hospital has been in the black for years and has managed to deliver decent care to everyone, rich and poor, for decades.

MARTY: Decent care! And that's how we got to be 48th out of 50 states? (*Pauses.*) No! The state system is finished. This army of sullen, inefficient civil servants, sucking off the tit of the state, is going to have to face the music. They can work with the private sector, which may even be not-for-profit I might add, or retire, or just go home and hate me from there. They can't dislike me any more than they already do. To hell with them all!

DR. PEACH: There are still ways to reform the system, improve it and make it more efficient. We don't want to throw the babies out with the bathwater.

MARTY: Clever, Dr. Peach, but I'm not interested in improving a broken system. I want the state out of the healthcare delivery business. And you, Dr. Peach, have demonstrated your persistent opposition to change. Since everyone is either part of the solution or part of the problem, you have demonstrated that you are part of the problem. Dr. Peach, you're fired!

DR. PEACH: But. . . .

MARTY: But what? You are an unclassified employee who serves at the discretion of the governor. That's me! And my discretion is that you leave your position immediately.

TONY: Should I call security, sir?

DR. PEACH: Don't bother. It's been my pleasure to serve. I hope my successor will continue to have the best interest of the people of this state at heart.

MARTY: (*Laughs.*) Like you? Sucking off the tit of the state while cranking out piss-poor health statistics. Give me a break, doctor.

TONY: Should I show the doctor out?

MARTY: Please do. (*To DR. PEACH.*) The people of this state need jobs, good paying, tax-producing jobs, not charity. Prosperity brings good health, not unemployment. We can never spend our way to good health.

DR. PEACH: Yes, we need good jobs, but companies will come to a state not only because of tax breaks and lax regulations, but also because of a healthy and well-educated workforce, which doesn't exist here at this time.

MARTY: Don't you dare lecture me! I'm the elected representative of the people and you are nothing! (*Yells.*) GET OUT!

DR. PEACH: And as the so-called champion of healthcare and education, you have sadly missed the mark.

TONY: I'm calling security.

MARTY: (*To TONY.*) Do it! And get this radical, tax-and-spend socialist out of my sight. He's making me physically sick.

DR. PEACH: I'm leaving. (*Exits.*)

TONY: He's a good doctor. He treated my brother, you know, and discovered that he suffered from some rare disease that no one else had diagnosed. My whole family loves the guy.

MARTY: That's nice. I'm sure he'll be able to use his talents elsewhere, the further from this state the better.

TONY: I thought you wanted our citizens to be able to get jobs in this state and not have to leave.

MARTY: Shut up! Bring me those files about the oil spill, and that damn sinkhole, too. And don't forget those papers about the brain-eating amoebas. Now those are real problems that need looking into.

TONY: Yes, sir.

MARTY: And don't forget to bring me that cup of herbal tea. All this arguing gives me a headache. I need something to soothe my nerves.

SCENE III - LE RENCONTRE (THE MEETING)

(HUBERT and MARTY enter from opposite sides of an empty stage. They meet in the middle.)

MARTY: *(Looks closely at HUBERT.)* Hubert?

HUBERT: Yes.

MARTY: *(Extends his right hand to HUBERT.)* Nice to meet you. I've read a lot about you. I'm Marty.

HUBERT: *(Shakes MARTY's hand.)* Nice to meet you. *(Looks closely at MARTY.)* Do I know you?

MARTY: Probably not. You were way before my time. *(Looks around.)* Where are we, anyway?

HUBERT: *(Sighs.)* I'm not really sure. *(Leans closer to MARTY.)* I think we're in purgatory.

MARTY: Purgatory! *(Looks around.)* You've got to be kidding.

HUBERT: No, I'm not.

MARTY: I can image why you might be here, but me? That's ridiculous. I've been devotedly religious all my life, a very good Catholic. There really must be some mistake.

HUBERT: What's that supposed to mean?

MARTY: Well, you were a philandering, power-hungry, populist prick, and probably agnostic as well. Does that about sum it up?

HUBERT: That's harsh. And by the way, I'm a Southern Baptist, at least officially.

MARTY: And you left our state in a hell of a mess. It took me eight years to wipe away all that socialist garbage you started 70 years ago.

HUBERT: What exactly did you do?

MARTY: What didn't I do? That's more like it. First, I closed Grand Caritas Hospital, wiped out the state-run health system, well, privatized it is more like it. Second, I fired half of the state's sullen civil servants. And third, I tried to change the pension system that's destroying the state, even though that didn't work out as well as I'd hoped. Oh, and I also helped give school vouchers to poor black kids so they could get out of failing schools. Now that was a catfight.

HUBERT: You closed Grand Caritas Hospital?

MARTY: You bet, with a little help from Katrina.

HUBERT: Katrina who?

MARTY: Hurricane Katrina. (*Shrugs.*) That's recent history. You wouldn't know about that, would you?

(*A silence ensues.*)

HUBERT: (*Attacks MARTY and tries to strangle him.*) You pompous little son-of-a-bitch! I'll beat the crap outta you.

(*MARTY and HUBERT struggle. MARTY manages to free himself and pull away.*)

MARTY: You crazy old man! Leave me alone!

HUBERT: Where will they go for care?

MARTY: Who?

HUBERT: The poor people?

MARTY: (*Sighs and shrugs.*) To the private sector, of course. The private sector will take care of the poor.

HUBERT: (*Shakes his head.*) There weren't enough private doctors to see the poor in my day. I can't imagine that's changed that much since then. Besides, there ain't enough money in the world to make the private docs see the poor. And there are just too many poor people all over the state to be taken care of.

MARTY: (*Strikes a pose.*) Remember, Jesus said, "The poor ye shall always have among you." (*Pauses.*) And they're still there, just more of them than back in your day, lots more.

HUBERT: You're cold!

MARTY: No, just practical. (*Pauses.*) You can't build a prosperous society on the dredges. We have to wager on the strong, the industrious, and the entrepreneurial.

HUBERT: The rich, you mean.

MARTY: Precisely, the rich. And there's nothing wrong with that. We want to build on the wealthy, good companies that bring good jobs, good wages, and insurance coverage. A rising tide floats all ships, you know.

HUBERT: Yeah, but it drowns the ones without boats. (*Shakes his head.*) How could you close Grand Caritas Hospital?

MARTY: How could I not? You left a cesspool of costly, inefficient, unproductive healthcare delivery. It was separate but unequal care and they got rid of that in the sixties. You might have been able to live with that, but I was not! You and I are very different people.

HUBERT: No, we're not.

MARTY: How so?

HUBERT: Because we both wanted the same thing anyway.

MARTY: What? The good of the people?

HUBERT: No, we wanted power.

MARTY: No, I wanted to change society and turn it back to its basic roots: Christian values, industry, thrift, private enterprise and personal responsibility.

HUBERT: (*Yells.*) You're a liar! You're cynical, immoral and hypocritical, that's what you are! You'll build your fool's paradise on the bones of the poor and helpless and call it progress. Cynical, immoral and hypocritical!

MARTY: No, I'm not! And don't you dare use my words against me! Keeping the poor in ignorance, poverty and sickness is really what's cynical, immoral and hypocritical. You were all three, not me! I am the healthcare governor! I am the education governor! I am the savior of the state!

HUBERT: Liar! I could hear the moans and groans of the people all the way into this God-forsaken place. (*Points to MARTY.*) You're goin' rot here, Marty, my friend. You're goin' rot here for a millennium while you dwell on your sins.

MARTY: Crazy old man! Shut up! Maybe this is purgatory if I have to listen to the likes of you for days, weeks, years. . . .

HUBERT: How about decades, maybe centuries.

MARTY: (*Looks around.*) Oh shit.

(*MARTY and HUBERT stand in silence, lost in their thoughts.*)

HUBERT: Did you finally get it?

MARTY: Get what?

HUBERT: What you wanted?

MARTY: What was that?

HUBERT: Power.

MARTY: (*Thinks.*) Yes, I did get power, lots of it.

HUBERT: And money?

MARTY: Enough. But that was never the goal, just a means to an end.

HUBERT: You see, (*Slaps MARTY on the back*) we're not that different. That was my feeling exactly.

MARTY: Spare me the details, old man.

HUBERT: No, it's true. That's what made me so dangerous to other politicians in my time.

MARTY: Yes, destroying free enterprise with your taxes and entitlements.

HUBERT: No, not that. I mean our President back in my day wasn't afraid of anyone but me, a Southern populist who wasn't corrupt. (*Spins around.*) I never cared about the money. It was just like Bible says.

MARTY: (*Holds up hid hand.*) Please, enough pontificating.`

HUBERT: No, really! Jesus also said, "Seek you first the Kingdom of Heaven and all things will be given unto you."

MARTY: Stop it!

HUBERT: Our Kingdom of Heaven was power and we both got everythin' else we needed as an added bonus.

MARTY: (*Thinks.*) Except perhaps love.

HUBERT: The people loved me! There were so many folks at my funeral that they filled the whole huge garden in front of the state buildin'. There were men and women and children, rich ones, poor ones, people in suits and overalls. They cried and wept while they trampled the landscapin' and just about destroyed the place. Hubert, Hubert, Hubert! You should've seen it. It was a real testimony to the love of the people for me.

MARTY: I read it was more like a circus.

HUBERT: They loved me. I was the governor for the little people from the swamps to the piney woods. I was their governor and the governor of the rich ones, too. Even the fat cats got used to me in the end. (*Pauses.*) What about you?

MARTY: (*Sadly.*) I think I was more feared than loved.

HUBERT: A Machiavellian, eh?

MARTY: What do you mean?

HUBERT: Machiavelli wrote, "It was better to be feared than loved to stay in power." Was that it with you?

MARTY: Something like that.

HUBERT: Must've been real lonely.

MARTY: Sometimes. But power, especially the heights of power, is always lonely. It's the burden of leadership and I was willing to shoulder it.

HUBERT: Did you make it?

MARTY: Where?

HUBERT: To the summit of power, to the presidency?

MARTY: No, sadly I did not. (*Pauses.*) It surely wasn't for lack of trying. I did everything to follow the pure dogma of the party. I was an unblemished lamb of conservatism, without a trace of personal scandal. I never supported a new tax. I never had an affair. And yet it was never enough, not for the big prize. (*Looks at HUBERT.*) What happened? Why did it slip between my fingers when it seemed so close?

HUBERT: (*Shrugs.*) Don't ask me. (*Pauses.*) I built hospitals, roads, schools and the mother of all political power bases and someone killed me anyway.

MARTY: Yes, I read about it. A tough way to go.

HUBERT: The little shit who killed me was a doctor, no less, an ear nose and throat specialist of all things. (*Pauses.*) You can trust the little people, but you always have to watch out for the educated elites. They'll stab you in the back every time.

MARTY: I love the elites. (*Pauses.*) Well, maybe not the educated ones, but at least the rich ones, the captains of industry and commerce. I loved them all.

HUBERT: But they didn't love your back, did they?

MARTY: (*Sighs.*) No, they didn't. I always felt just a wee bit on the outside, even in those power-packed back rooms.

HUBERT: (*Goes over and give MARTY a big hug.*) No one loved you, did they?

MARTY: My wife and family did.

HUBERT: Well that's somethin', anyway. But it doesn't count in politics.

MARTY: And God loves me? Doesn't he?

HUBERT: (*Looks around at the emptiness.*) Apparently not. Not if he put you in this place. (*Pauses.*) Hey, since we have gotta lot of time on our hands, how about havin' some fun?

MARTY: (*Skeptical.*) Like what?

(*HUBERT takes MARTY in dance position.*)

HUBERT: Can you dance?

MARTY: (*Stammers.*) No, not really. I never had the time for that.

HUBERT: It's easy. A polka step is just one-two-three hop, two-two-three hop. First one way and then the other. And then we can spin around a bit.

(*MARTY follows and they begin to dance. They accelerate with time and then stop.*)

HUBERT: Good! Very good! You're a natural. Now, with music? Ready?

MARTY: This isn't very dignified. What if someone sees us dancing? A man dancing with another man might be misinterpreted. It might cause a scandal, show up on YouTube or something, you know.

HUBERT: U-tube?

MARTY: Cell phones, videos, everyone's always looking. (*Pauses.*) Forget it.

HUBERT: (*Looks around.*) So who's watching? And who cares anyway? (*Swings his arms around.*) Not a soul in any direction.

MARTY: (*Looks around.*) Okay. (*Pause.*) And by the way, thanks for teaching me to dance. It's a nice thing to do. I never had a lot of real friends. It might be nice.

HUBERT: My pleasure. (*Pauses.*) This music was well known, something some governor wrote between you and me. It's just one-two-three-hop. Very easy. (*Shouts.*) Start the music!

(*"You are my Sunshine," starts to play. It is a 4/4 rhythm and is good for a polka. MARTY and HUBERT dance together. They smile and laugh as the lights dim to dark.*)

THE END

A LAST DANCE

LEARNING KUCMOCH

(Pronounced Koos-mock, with the accent on the first syllable.)

CAST OF CHARACTERS

DANIEL: Dance instructor. No particular accent.

BARBARA: Daniel's dance partner. She has a foreign accent, but not Slavic.

CHARLIE: Middle-aged man with a marked Southern rural accent.

YARMILLA: Middle-aged woman of Czech descent, but with a marked Southern rural accent.

SETTING

The setting is a dance hall, with four chairs off to the side. Daniel is teaching the others a Czech dance, Kucmoch (originally taught by Jitka Bonusova of the dance group Dvorana in Prague.)

DANIEL: Okay, the music's starting. (*Starts a CD player.*)

(*Kucmoch begins. It is a cheerful Czech dance melody with alternating polka and waltz melodies. It is a couple-dance and DANIEL is dancing with BARBARA and CHARLIE is dancing with YARMILLA. There are eight set-hops, followed by four waltz steps and the man turns the woman under his arm with a flourish.*)

DANIEL: No! (*Stops the CD player.*) Let's try that again. Yarmilla, you're leading poor Charlie and neither of you are following the melody.

CHARLIE: (*Laughs.*) I thought I was doin' pretty good.

DANIEL: (*Frowns.*) Yes, pretty good. (*Pauses.*) I know you have bad knees, but the rhythm is still there and you need to try and make at least one full turn as a couple. (*To YARMILLA.*) Your turn under Charlie's arm looked very good. A nice flourish.

YARMILLA: Well, at least there's somethin' good about what I do. (*Angrily.*) Why can't we just do some of the old dances we already know? What's the point of killin' ourselves learnin' a complicated new dance when we know dozens of old dances already?

DANIEL: It's not killing anyone, is it? (*Gestures around the room.*) I don't see any corpses yet.

YARMILLA: Yeah, but it's a lot of work and Charlie's in pain and so is Barbara in case you haven't noticed.

DANIEL: (*To BARBARA.*) Are you in pain?

BARBARA: Yes, I am. I have pain in my right hip and it's hard to make turns without really hurting. This dance is full of turns.

DANIEL: (*Exasperated.*) There aren't that many geriatric Czech folk dances. Besides, we just aren't that old and debilitated yet.

CHARLIE: Speak for yourself. My body's a wreck. Look at my knees. (*Pulls up his pant to reveal his hairy legs.*)

DANIEL: Okay, they do look pretty bad. Let's take a break and talk about the costumes we're going to wear for the performance.

(*All four pull chairs forward and make an open semi-circle center stage forward.*)

DANIEL: So what about the costumes?

YARMILLA: I don't know about you, Barbara, but I'm wearin' the traditional costume, the red skirt and the black vest.

BARBARA: The blue skirt and the green vest from Moravia are so much nicer. They're also authentic, the real thing from the Old World.

YARMILLA: Real thing! They're just imported clothes, not our traditional homegrown costumes.

BARBARA: Real and traditional! Yarmilla, since when are sequined eagles and maps of Louisiana the real thing? That's about as made-up as you can get. It's fake, not traditional.

YARMILLA: Fake! You're the fake ones, wearin' clothes that aren't even in our heritage and dancin' dances that you never learned as a child. That's fake. That's stealin' someone else's culture.

DANIEL: It doesn't matter! We can each wear whatever costume you want, the local version or the imported one.

BARBARA: At least the imported ones actually come from the Old World and look beautiful.

YARMILLA: If you don't like our costumes, just don't wear them. Or better yet, go back to the Old World and leave us alone and let us wear whatever we want. Make us feel good for a change and don't put us down all the time like we are your dumb country relatives and you're the lords of the land, playin' with the native children.

CHARLIE: Come on, Yarmilla. Cool it! This is supposed to be a fun activity. Folk dancing is supposed to bring us all together in a happy group around our common heritage. And that included people we welcome here. What's the point of fighting about it? It's ridiculous.

DANIEL: Back to the costumes, please. What about the men's shirts? (*To CHARLIE.*) You want to wear the local one or the imported one.

YARMILLA: He should wear the local, of course.

BARBARA: Imported!

DANIEL: Charlie, what do you want to wear? After all, it's only the two of us men anyway.

CHARLIE: To tell you the truth, I've gained so much weight that I can't get into my into the shirt my mama made me, local or not. Stuffed into that shirt, I look like a hairy Czech sausage and it ain't pretty.

DANIEL: So we go with the new, imported shirts for the guys. (*Looks at YARMILLA and BARBARA.*) Is that okay with you, ladies?

BARBARA and YARMILLA: Yes.

DANIEL: Okay, now what about the choice of dances for the performance.

YARMILLA: I say we do the old dances that we already know and call it quits. Learnin' anything new at this point in time is ridiculous. Look at Charlie; he's almost a cripple. He can barely move, much less do fancy new steps. (*Pauses. To DANIEL.*) Have some mercy. Let's just stick with the old, easy dances, please. Nothin' new.

BARBARA: My hip hurts, too. But I think I can manage Kucmoch. It's a nice dance and it's not that hard, except for the turns.

YARMILLA: I didn't say it wasn't nice, I just said it's new and we don't need new.

CHARLIE: I think I can do it, too. There's not that much jumping and no kneeling. I can't kneel down and get back up.

DANIEL: (*Looks at YARMILLA.*) You okay with that?

YARMILLA: Okay, but this is the last new dance we learn.

DANIEL: So let's work on it. Everyone up and in couples.

> (*All rise and replace their chairs to the periphery of the stage. DANIEL and BARBARA form a couple and CHARLIE and YARMILLA.*)

DANIEL: Now the men skip forward and the women skip backwards. The guys clap, then the women clap on alternating beats. Clap guys, clap girls, clap guys, clap girls. (*Demonstrates with BARBARA.*) Then give left hands and pass twice with two waltz steps so you end face to face. (*Demonstrates with BARBARA.*) Then do the penguin turns twice and four running steps to end face to face. (*Demonstrates with BARBARA.*)

CHARLIE: I can't remember all that.

YARMILLA: I'll push and pull you through, don't worry.

CHARLIE: I don't want you pushing me! You're pushy enough already. Let me sit this one out. My knees hurt and so does my head.

DANIEL: (*Pushes BARBARA forward.*) Here, Charlie, dance with Barbara. She's pretty gentle and she won't lead you, I promise.

BARBARA: Pretty gentle? That's insulting. Of course I'm gentle, very gentle.

DANIEL: Sorry, very gentle. I'll dance with Yarmilla.

YARMILLA: Maybe I don't want to dance with you. You don't even belong to this community. You're an intruder, an interloper, an an alien invader. You drop out of nowhere and start teachin' dances right from the Old World. Maybe you outta to go back where you came from and leave us in peace. We left the Old World and maybe it's better that way. You're just importin' discord, not harmony. We were fine before you got here and we'll be fine when you're long gone.

CHARLIE: Stop it! Daniel and Barbara have worked with us for years. It's beautiful what they've brought. It's made us all better. It's brought us together. (*Pauses.*) Can we help it if the young people don't care anymore and that the dance materiel is too hard? Can we help it if we are just too old and sick to jump around? Can they help it that we want to stick to just what we had before and no more. (*Takes BARBARA.*) Come on. I'll dance with you if you'll have me. But be warned that I'm rather dangerous on the dance floor.

(*All form couples.*)

BARBARA: (*To CHARLIE.*) Just please don't step on my feet. You're too fat and you'll break them.

CHARLIE: Well, more and more compliments. (*Takes BARBARA.*) You'd think that folk dancing would be immune to this sort of bickering. It's supposed to be fun and bring people together in happiness. It's supposed to recreate that beautiful little village in the mist, that Brigadoon along the Red River. (*To all.*) Can't we just all get along!

DANIEL: (*Laughs.*) Right, Rodney King! (*Pauses.*) I wish there were a happy little village where people danced in peace. (*Pauses.*) Nothing's immune from bickering, not even folk dancing. Can we continue with the practice?

YARMILLA: (*Sighs.*) Okay, I'm sorry for being so unpleasant. I've got a lot on my mind and this just doesn't seem to help anymore. I'd like to lose myself in that village, too, that place where everyone gets along but I'm not sure ever existed. (*Pauses.*) I'll be okay when the music starts. Let's dance . . . for the good of the group.

DANIEL: Yes, for the good of the group. Ready. Music! (*Presses on a CD player.*)

> (*Kucmoch plays and the dancers complete the second figure, ending with a bow to one another. Lights dim to dark.*)

THE END

ABOUT THE AUTHOR

Dr. David Holcombe was born and raised in the San Francisco Bay Area. After attending the University of California at Davis and the University of Florida in Gainesville, he left the United States and attended medical school at the Catholic University of Louvain in Brussels, Belgium. While teaching folk dancing classes there to earn some income, he met his future wife, Nicole Catherine.

After returning to the United States in 1983, Dr. Holcombe did a residency in internal Medicine at a Johns-Hopkins affiliated clinic in Baltimore. He and his wife and first son, Renaud, settled in Alexandria, Louisiana in 1986, where they have remained and raised three other children, Tanguy, Joffroi and Thibault.

Dr. Holcombe remains a prolific, if unrecognized, author. A dozen of his short plays have been produced in the context of Spectral Sisters Productions in Alexandria, Louisiana, over the last decade. There is a disturbing incisiveness in his works that sometimes evokes discomfort in readers and viewers alike, but which reflects the depth of his vision. His medical career has always offered a unique window into the extraordinary complexity of human behavior, sometimes admirable and sometimes appalling.

Writing and medicine have co-existed somewhat uneasily over the years in Dr. Holcombe's life. Much like Thomas Mann's character, Tonio Kruger, Dr. Holcombe has found himself caught between the scientific and literary worlds, too much in both to be completely in one or the other. This life-long tension produces some of the most unique and vibrant literary works of our troubled times, a kaleidoscope of personalities and issues. The creative spirit continues to flourish in him, however, with or without recognition, in a most unlikely location.